INSIGHT POCKET GUIDES

THE FRENCH RIVIERA

CW00358260

APA PUBLICATIONS
Part of the Langenscheidt Publishing Group

L

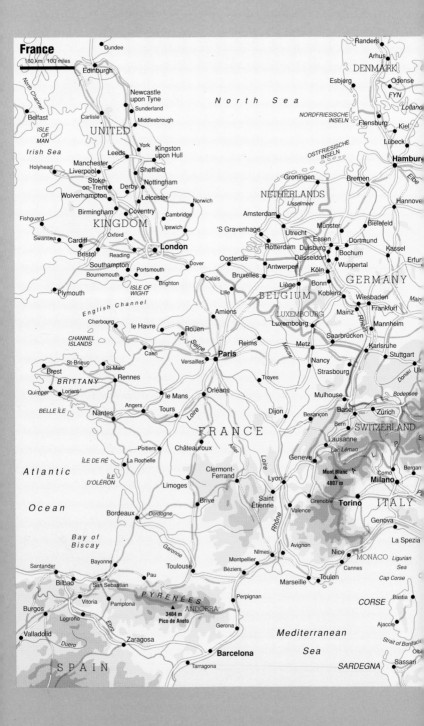

Welcome!

In 1887 the French poet Stephen Liègard wrote a book about France's Mediterranean coast and called it *La Côte d'Azur*. Thus the French Riviera gained its name. This azure-blue coast is associated with some of the 20th century's greatest painters and writers; with fashionable Cannes, Monte Carlo and St Tropez; with high society, glamour and the stuff of which dreams are made.

In these pages Insight Guides' correspondent on the the French Riviera, Michaela Lentz, brings you the best of the region. Twenty-two itineraries are based on five key areas: Nice and environs; the coastline between Nice and Menton; the hinterland between Nice and Vence; St-Paul-de-Vence to Cannes; and Cannes to St-Tropez. They can be followed individually or linked to make a grand tour. Following the itineraries is an introduction to the region's food and wine, a calendar of special events and festivals, and a detailed practical information section.

Michaela Lentz first visited the French Riviera in 1951, when she was fortunate enough to visit Picasso in his studio in Vallauris. The experience triggered a lasting love for the region and drew her back time and time again. Eventually she came to stay, setting up home in an old farmhouse near Vence, where she writes novels, cookery books and children's books. Although she has seen many changes over the years (as she says, 'the Côte d'Azur is loved too well by too many not to change'), her passion hasn't waned at all. In this guide, her aim is to pass it on to you.

C O N T E N T S

Pages 2/3:
Jardin
Exotique, Eze

Pages 8/9:
On the beach in
St Tropez

HISTORY

Sun and Sand, Ships and Shore

In the Grotto of Vallonet, near Roquebrune, archaeologists have found tools estimated to be around 900,000 years old – the oldest in France. Historical records date back to around 1000BC when a broad stretch of the Mediterranean coast was settled by the Ligurians. In 600BC Greeks from Phocaea in Asia Minor founded what is now Marseille, planting the land with olive, fig, nut and cherry trees and grape vines, and introducing the use of money. The city quickly prospered under these excellent traders, who went on to establish trading posts in Hyères, St Tropez, Antibes, Nice and Monaco.

Attracted by the wealth, the Celts lost no time before invading Provence, where they intermarried with the Ligurians. In 125BC Marseille appealed to Rome for help in ousting these invaders. Within three years the Romans had not only freed Marseille but conquered the whole Mediterranean region, going on to capture Aix from the Teutons in 102BC. During the first century BC Marseille supported Pompey, Caesar's rival. Caesar was victorious and removed power to Arles and Fréjus. When Caesar died, the Alps were still occupied by 44 unconquered tribes. Augustus finally succeeded in

bringing them under Roman rule, and to commemorate the victory, in 6BC a 130ft (40m) monument was built at the foot of Mont Agel, at the meeting-point of the Via Julia and other major roads constructed during the battles. This Alpine Trophy still stands to this day at La Turbie, by Monaco.

The Via Aurelia (which followed much the same course as today's N7) was one of the most important thoroughfares in the Roman Empire.

It connected Rome with Arles by way of Genoa, Cimiez (Nice), Antibes, Fréjus and Aix. Every Roman mile (4,850ft/1,478m) there were marker stones indicating the distances (one of these marker stones can be examined in the museum in St Raphael). Cimiez was then the administrative capital of the *Alpes Maritimae*. Excavations there convey an idea of the highly developed culture of the Romans.

The uncontested rule of the Romans brought the region a period of peace (the *Pax Romana*) which lasted until Provence was invaded in turn by the Vandals, Visigoths, Burgundians, Ostragoths and Franks in the 5th and 6th centuries. The Saracens, Moorish pirates, arrived from Spain and settled in the Massif des Maures behind Grimaud. They were expelled in 973 after terrorising the region for over 100 years, but they continued looting coastal areas until well into the 18th century.

Roman ruins at Cimiez

Provence, declared a kingdom by Lothaire, King of the Franks, in 855, was made part of the Holy Roman Empire in the 10th century, although the Counts of Provence retained considerable independence. Two hundred years later Provence fell first into the hands of the Counts of Toulouse and then the Counts of Barcelona, and in 1246 went to the House of Anjou when Charles of Anjou married the daughter of the Count of Barcelona. In 1308 the Grimaldi family purchased Monaco from the Genoans.

Toward the middle of the 14th century, plague ravaged Europe, decimating populations. The southern coast of France was not spared. After the death of the Queen of Sicily (revered as 'Pure Jeanne' by the people of Provence), the French House of Anjou and the King of Naples contended over who should rule Provence. Nice voted for the King of Naples, although he was not able to guarantee the city any effective protection. Count Amadeus VII from the Savoy exploited this situation. As a result, in 1388 Nice and its hinterland left Provence to become part of the Duchy of Savoy in Italy, where it remained, on and off, until 1860. In contrast, the region to the west of the River Var remained a part of Provence, and became French in 1486. The area known today as the Côte d'Azur thus consisted of two regions from the Middle Ages until the 18th century. During this time violent confrontations between the two were frequent. In 1860, the Duchy of Nice was finally incorporated into France.

The Casino at Monte Carlo

The First Tourists

In 1864 the PLM (Paris-Lyon-Mediterranean) railway line was extended to Nice, heralding the arrival of what was to become a thriving tourist industry. The region became the winter destination of kings and queens, aristocrats and politicians, courtesans, actors and actresses, musicians and artists. In 1887 the French poet Stephen Liègard entitled his book about France's Mediterranean coast *La Côte d'Azur*, thus giving the landscape its name forever.

Nowadays the name Côte d'Azur conjures up images of sun and sand, yachts and beaches, intense colours, mild nights and heady scents, tanned skins and culinary delights. It was not always thus, however; foreign visitors used to come for the autumn, winter and spring, returning home to escape from the heat of the Mediterranean summer sun, which was considered unhealthy.

The British were largely responsible for discovering and developing the Riviera into what it is today. Cannes owes its fame to Lord Brougham, who settled there in 1834. Towards the end of the 19th century Queen Victoria, whose subjects had already financed the construction of the famous Promenade des Anglais in 1820, made Nice the 'Winter Capital of the British Empire'. Meanwhile St Tropez was being transformed into a painting centre by Paul Signac.

Queen Victoria would leave her yacht in Calais and board her private train, which would 'race' her down to Nice at 35 miles (55km) per hour. Her stay at the Hôtel Regina in Cimiez was the event of the year. Naturally, she entered the hotel through a private entrance exclusively reserved for her use, and she even had her own bed brought from London for the duration of her stay. She took great pleasure in touring the hinterland by coach. The proprietors of the simple country taverns and lodges in which she would stop to refresh herself en route were prepared for her arrival long ahead of time. Signs were hastily painted and prominently displayed with the promise: 'Five o'clock tea – any time of the day!'

The Belle Epoque lifestyle of the Côte d'Azur came to an end with World War I. The Royal Highnesses now had more important matters to attend to.

Between the Wars

The 1920s on the Côte d'Azur were the *années folles*, wanton and wild, and long before Fellini coined the expression, the millionaires were living a very *dolce vita*, especially Americans who were happy to escape from Prohibition. Cole Porter was one of the first to take up summer quarters, in a villa on the Cap d'Antibes. It was thanks to him that the rich American Gerald Murphy and his wife Sara came down from Paris on the *Train Bleu*. The next year, 1923, they rented a villa on the Cap and discovered the joys of swimming and sunbathing. The Murphys gathered a clique around themselves every summer in their Villa America and neighbouring villas, a clique which included Hemingway, Picasso, Léger, the Mistinguetts and, perhaps predictably, Scott and Zelda Fitzgerald.

In 1926, André Sella, owner of the Hôtel du Cap, was persuaded by his 'wild' clientele to open in the summertime. (The hotel still looks just as it did when Fitzgerald described it.) Soon convinced of the benefits of the new fashion for sun, Sella built the Eden Roc pavilion for sun-worshippers and swimmers next door to his hotel.

The beach at Cannes

The Lérins Islands

Erika Mann, the daughter of the Nobel prize-winner Thomas Mann (author of *The Magic Mountain*), later marvelled: 'The swimming-pool is quite unique, carved into the cliffs so that it has something of a rather pathetic grotto, with diving-boards at enormous heights – dizzying athletic equipment. The conditions of membership in this water sport club are very complicated and expensive. Above the swimming-bath there is a bar decorated in light green from which you can see nothing but the sea, so that you feel as if you're on a ship...'

From then on bronzed skin became fashionable and aristocratic manners gave way to 'expensive simplicity' – to this day the only possible maxim for life on the Côte d'Azur. In essence, this represented the beginning of the summer tourist industry on the French Riviera, a trend that gained ground in 1936 when the French government introduced paid holidays.

At around this time a newly married couple appeared in Cannes on their honeymoon: Frank and Florence Gould. Florence, who had left her native San Francisco after the 1906 earthquake, met her husband, a multi-millionaire and heir to a rail baron's estate, in Paris. On an outing the two discovered a pine grove and beach next to the little village of Juan-les-Pins. It was the famous *coup de foudre* which is reputed to have lasted for a lifetime. Florence not only bought all the land, she began to build on it immediately: first a casino and then the Hôtel Le Provençal, which was soon a serious rival to the Hôtel du Cap ('Oh, so distinguished' oozed the English advertising flyers). She also built a villa for herself and Frank which she transformed into a neo-Gothic castle. The Côte d'Azur has always inspired excess of one sort or another.

The Goulds received not only *le beau monde*, but also famed French authors of the time. Benoit, Gide, Morand, Montherlant, Giraudoux, Louise de Vilmorin, as well as Scott and Zelda Fitzgerald were, from 1924 on, among the guests who attended many wild and boisterous parties where the champagne flowed generously. This was the decade of Gatsby abroad, the era immortalised in such books as Fitzgerald's *Tender is the Night*.

For more than half a century the Goulds

Sophia Loren

ruled over Juan-les-Pins and Cannes, where they acquired Villa Le Patio. In rooms with splendid paintings on the walls by artists such as Van Gogh and Matisse, they entertained Film Festival stars and other prominent people: Sophia Loren, Ingrid Bergman, Picasso and Dalí, Maurice Chevalier and Françoise Sagan, René Clair and Orson Welles, Elizabeth Taylor and Richard Burton. In 1961 General de Gaulle honoured Mrs Gould for meritorious patronage. She died in 1983 aged 88.

Back to the year 1925. The famed Colette, of whom more anon, until then a staunch visitor to Brittany, fell in love with St Tropez. There she discovered for the first time the pleasures of the Midi. The author of *Claudine in Paris* and *Gigi* invited her friends to her house (La Treille Muscate, situated in the middle of a vineyard), and visitors included such distinguished personalities as Lucien Guitry, Dunoyer de Segonzac, Jean-Pierre Aumont, Jeff Kessel, Saint Exupéry, Cocteau, Simone Simon and Marc Allégret. By 1936 the tourists and photographers were getting on her nerves, and

Who is the fairest on the beach?

Colette sold her house in St Tropez. From then on, whenever she visited her beloved Midi, she stayed with friends in Grasse or in the Hôtel de Paris in Monte Carlo.

Romance Blooms

In 1930 a tall and very slim young woman called Yvette, who lived in Cannes with her parents, was selected as 'Miss France'. Not far from the fashion salon in which Yvette worked, the Aga Khan, who frequently visited Cannes, was amusing himself playing skittles. However, the fateful meeting of the two did not take place on the Croisette, but rather eight years later in Cairo. Yvette became 'The Begum', one of the richest women in the world. The couple lived in Le Cannet in the Villa Yakimour – *Y* for Yvette, *mour* as in

15

The Hôtel de Paris in Monte Carlo

amour! There was scarcely a party on the Côte that the two didn't attend. After the death of her husband in 1957, Yvette largely withdrew from the hubbub, dedicating herself to painting and sculpture, though for years afterwards she could still often be seen walking in the streets of Cannes, reminding many who knew of her about the wonderful days gone by.

In December 1936, some 200 international journalists awaited the arrival of Wallis Simpson, the American woman who, as the world was shortly to find out, was worth more to a king than his throne. On 12 December 1936 King Edward VIII abdicated, saying that he did not feel that he was able to fulfil his duties as monarch without the help and support of the woman he loved. With tears in her eyes the twice-divorced Wallis listened to this declaration of love in her Villa Viei. Six months later the couple were married. In the Château de la Croë on the Cap d'Antibes the Duke and Duchess of Windsor led a luxurious life in exile. At the beginning of World War II they left the Château, not returning until 1945.

War and After

World War II kept visitors away from the Riviera. Nice's historical links with Italy inspired Mussolini to bring the south-eastern tip of France 'home' to Italy, and the Italians occupied Menton in 1940. After the split between Germany and Italy in 1943, the Germans took over the occupation. The Resistance movement was active in the region, repatriating escaped prisoners and shot-down air crews. Allied troops liberated Provence in August 1944, landing

View of Menton

on the beaches between Toulon and the Esterel. Sir Winston Churchill watched the landing from the destroyer *Kimberley* off Pampelonne Beach near St Tropez.

In 1946 Picasso came to live in Antibes, where he painted as if possessed. His large-scale work named *Joie de Vivre* said it all – the war was finally over, the pleasures of life were wll and truly back. At the beginning of the 1950s Picasso busied himself intensively with the war theme. He transformed the Roman chapel in Vallauris into a monument to peace with his work *La Guerre et la Paix* (War and Peace).

Picasso was not the only artist at work here in the 1950s. Matisse was working on the chapel in Vence; Chagall painted his *Messages Bibliques*. St Tropez, already in vogue with the Parisian literary circles, welcomed its most famous resident: Brigitte Bardot. Before long the less pleasant consequences of her meteoric rise became apparent. Brigitte was no longer able to go for walks along the harbour or go shopping in the narrow alleyways of the town without being whistled at or harassed by tourists. They even showed up in boats, drifting past her villa La Madrague in order to get a glimpse of their idol or snatch a photograph. Fatigued by her own mystique, Bardot even attempted suicide.

In Memoriam, Antibes

DOR DE LA SOUCHERE
MONTEE
1888 - 1977
FONDATEUR ET CONSERVATEUR
DU MUSEE PICASSO
DE 1926 A 1977

In Monaco, Prince Rainier III orientated the Principality's economy towards the American example – commercialising caviar and hot-dogs to the same degree. He also gained the love and support of a woman who gave up a successfu career as an actress to marry him in 1956. As Grace Kelly she was a major star in Hollywood; however, she played her biggesty and brightest role in Monaco.

Modern Development

Since then, there is no doubt that the times and the Côte d'Azur have changed. The Promenade des Anglais is now a superhighway. Those who wish to visit St Tropez (and cannot afford to rent a helicopter) will get stuck for hours in the traffic jams. The railway tracks no longer belong to the private trains of the upper crust, but rather to the fastest train in the western world: the TGV speeds along at 170 miles (270km) per hour. Once the Côte d'Azur was the playground of the happy few; now approximately 18 million tourists visit here annually.

Tourism has made the region famous, brought affluence, and defined its modern face. It's the basis of the economy. But business

The Harbour at St Tropez

and congress tourism is becoming ever more extensive, with hotel beds now filled in the off-season as well.

In an attempt to avoid the monoculture of tourism the Côte has decided to encourage non-polluting high-tech industry to establish bases there. Projects which reflect this decision include the research centre of the American information-processing giant IBM in La Gaude and the ambitious Sophia Antipolis science park near Valbonne, Europe's leading technology park. The brainchild of Senator Pierre Lafitte during the late 60s, who wanted to create a European Silicon Valley, Sophia Antipolis is a 12,000-acre (5,000 hectare) forested plateau dedicated to research and development, high technology and further education. Multinational corporations on the site include Digital, Dow Corning, Dow Chemical and Wellcome. Another international project, Amadeus, was created by Air France, SAS, Iberia and Lufthansa to centralise their reservation system. Amadeus has its marketing and software development headquarters in Sophia Antipolis.

Money is also being poured into luxury real-estate. The Villa Trianon on Cap Ferrat cost the late Christina Onassis 800,000 francs in rent per month. The Fabris, Rizzolis and Mondadoris have bought into the Cap as well. Price per villa? Between 20 and 30 million US dollars. Because his Villa Estella seemed too small in comparison with the Hôtel du Cap on the Cap d'Antibes, Greek tycoon John Latsis bought 40 additional acres (16 hectares) of land with buildings.

Princess Caroline

These few examples illustrate the scale of the development that has taken place in the region. Even so, there is considerably more to the French Riviera than the bravura of the coastal strip. Coast and hinterland are two extremes which nonetheless have a unity in their contrasts. It is precisely these contrasts which make a visit here a unique experience. It doesn't matter how you define the word vacation – there's something here which will please you.

18

The Balls Keep Rolling

The call *Faites vos jeux! Rien ne va plus* was heard for the first time in Monaco in 1856. Since then many have succumbed to a fascination with the little tumbling ball. Some, from superstition, picked up a few cheap postcards in the shop opposite the Casino before coming in and 'inadvertently' stroking them over the owner's humped back (a peculiar tradition thought sure to bring good luck). When the 'humpback' died, he left behind a considerable fortune, including his fake humps, which hung from a chair on leather straps.

Winston Churchill made his first appearance in the Casino in 1939. He returned in 1949 and, playing at the same table as 10 years before, won 2 million francs, all the while puffing away at his eternal cigar.

Casinos

Cannes

CASINO CROISETTE
Tel: 93 38 12 11. Open 11am (slot machines), gambling from 7pm. 50FF admission.

CARLTON CASINO CLUB
Tel: 93 68 00 33. Opens 7.30pm. 70FF admission

St Maxime

CASINO
Tel: 94 96 12 96.
Open 9pm–5am (closed in winter).

Nice

CASINO RUHL
Tel: 93 87 95 87. Open 8pm–4am. Also slot machines from 10am. 75FF admission to roulette.

Monte Carlo

LOEWS CASINO
Tel: 93 50 65 00.
Open 11am (slot machines) and from 5pm gambling room.

MONTE CARLO CASINO
Tel: 92 16 21 21. 50FF admission. Salle Europe opens at noon; Salle Blanche, Salon des Amérique, Salon Rose at 2pm; Salons Privés at 4pm.

Antibes/Juan-les-Pins

EDEN BEACH CASINO
Tel: 92 93 71 71. Open from 8pm. 70FF admission to roulette.

Mandelieu La Napoule

ROYAL HOTEL CASINO
Tel: 92 97 70 00.
Open 9pm–5am. 75FF admission.

'Boules' under discussion

The balls are still rolling thanks in particular to wealthy Italian guests from Turin and Milan. Meanwhile, banks of one-armed bandits have also been installed. Tourists can try their luck on these in the afternoons – sometimes even in the morning. Slot machines at such venues as the Casino Ruhl and Monte Carlo Casino open at 10am.

A little ball, called *le but* or *le bouchon*, also plays a considerable role in the most popular game of Southern France. In earlier days *boules* or *pétanque* was played with wooden balls sheathed with nails; nowadays they are made of stainless steel. One of the players throws the smallest ball – the wooden *bouchon*, which is about 1in (25mm) in diameter – for a distance of up to 60ft (20m). With the next throw he tries to get his metal ball as close as he possibly can to the *bouchon*.

A player of the other team then strives to get his ball still closer. The opponents take turns in their endeavours. For each ball which is closer than that of the best of the opposing team, the player receives one point. The game is finished when one team has 15 points. The challenge of the game lies, in part, in the various techniques for manoeuvering a ball closer to the *bouchon*. You can roll the ball directly towards the little wooden ball, or you can shoot for an enemy ball to push it away from the *bouchon*. Finally, you can aim at the *bouchon* to push it away from an enemy ball or bring it closer to one of your own.

The game is all about the decisions that players must make before each toss: Should they aim? If yes, how? Is the track uneven, or does it have little stones on it which could influence the course of the ball? Such questions and the expected result of a toss are discussed at length over and over again. In essence, this is the attraction of the game – especially for the spectator. The perspicacity, humour, sarcasm, insults, arguments and curses with which the individual players dramatise every stage of play, and with luck outfox their opponents, are all part of a satisfactory game of *boules*. And the hollow, deep thwack of one ball hitting another remains one of the most evocative sounds of a warm summer evening on the Côte d'Azur.

From Bréa to César

The Nice School flourished between 1450 and 1570, a style of painting which can be compared in significance with that of Siena. The works of these painters, primarily employed by the Order of Penitent Monks, can be found in many of the pilgrimage churches and chapels in and around Nice, for example in Peille, Biot, Tourettes-sur-Loup, Bar-sur-Loup, Bouyon and Le Broc. The paintings and the buildings they ornament represent a lesser known facet of life on the Côte d'Azur, a sort of counterpoint for the purely sybaritic pleasures of sunning and dining.

The best known painter of altar images and frescoes from this period was Louis Bréa. He was born in Nice and was called the 'Provençal Fra Angelico', probably because of the naive uprightness, sincerity, humanity and simplicity with which he imbued his subjects. His brother Antoine, nephew François, Jean Miralheti, Jacques Durandi, Jean Canavesio, Jean Baleison and André de la Cella also belonged to *les primitifs niçois*.

In the 1950s and 1960s a second School of Nice came into being. Among its members are Arman, Ben, Chubac, Farhi, Gilly, Klein, Malaval, Morabito, Slobodan, Sosno and César.

Forest Fires

In the south of France – the so-called Midi – fire is the feared enemy of the forests. Most of the perpetrators can't be taken to court: they include the heat of summer, dryness, coniferous woods and underbrush, the unpredictable *Mistral* wind, carelessness and lack of investment in preventative measures. Added to this, however, is indeed a criminal aspect: some people start fires to benefit from insurance and some simply enjoy lighting fires.

In a recent typical three-year period in the six *départements* of the Provence-Côte d'Azur region there were eight deaths and 130 people were injured in fires. In the Midi there are more than 10 million acres (4 million hectares) of forest and underbrush which require protection. Attempts are being made to reduce the danger

of fire: underbrush is being cleared around residential areas and houses, fire breaks are being cut through the forest and patrols have been established for the early detection of flames.

Fire fighting is carried out by Canadair water-bombers, which are stationed in Marignane. The 'flying fire-department' logs somewhere in the region of 7,000 hours of flying time during the summer season, and the carefully chosen pilots risk their lives every day. They are masters of fire-fighting techniques and are able to unload their water tanks at a height of only 100ft (30m) above the ground.

The 'Angels of the Forest' are a group of young men – green-helmeted and equipped with walkie-talkies – who cover about 125 miles (200km) a day on motorcycles in endangered areas. Their mission is to detect fires early and observe visitors in the forest. The devastating spread of a forest fire can usually be prevented if the fire department can be called to the scene within the first 10 minutes. Since the establishment of the 'Green Helmets', pyromaniacs have not had such an easy time. But fire is now one of the greatest dangers throughout the entire Mediterranean basin, and visitors are asked to bear this in mind.

HOTEL DEVILLE

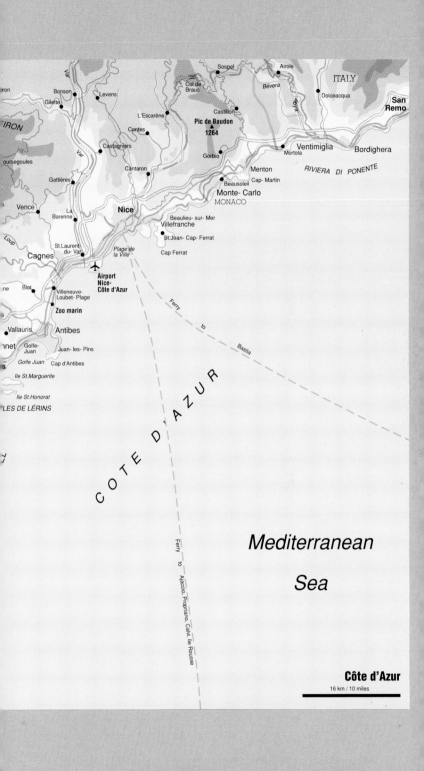

Côte d'Azur

16 km / 10 miles

Tours

The region covered by this guide is bordered by Menton in the east and St Tropez in the west. For the best overview of the area, use Michelin map 195.

Nice has been chosen as the point of departure for this book because it is the capital city of the French Riviera, as well as being the location of the international airport (the second-largest in France). Not by chance has this city become a major tourist centre and a gold mine for those seeking big-city diversions and activities.

If you like the fashionable life, Monte Carlo, the gambling capital of Europe, provides a unique milieu. Understated elegance awaits visitors to Beaulieu, Cap Ferrat, Cap Martin and Menton on the Basse Corniche, the coastal road from Nice to the Italian border. You can also reach Menton from Nice via the Moyenne Corniche, which has magnificent views over the sea and the coastal villages and is, moreover, the quickest route to Eze, one of the region's best preserved medieval mountain villages. Those interested in history might prefer the Grande Corniche, which partly follows the course of the ancient Via Julia Augusta, and gives you the chance to visit Roquebrune (a fortified town from the Carolingian period) and the famous Roman victory monument, the Alpine Trophy.

The route from Nice to Vence leads through hinterlands which have largely been spared from the hubbub of tourism. As well as giving a glimpse of some genuine Provençal countryside, it takes you to the Haute-de-Cagnes, where you can see Renoir's beautiful garden. Around Vence you can explore pure and charming landscapes and unspoiled mountain villages. The modern art

in the stylish Fondation Maeght should, if time and money allow, be followed by a meal at the legendary Colombe d'Or. Both are in St Paul-de-Vence and are unforgettable.

The drive from Nice to Cannes is rich with possibilities: the Escoffier Museum in Villeneuve-Loubet, the yachting harbour and Picasso museum in Antibes, a swim off the Cap d'Antibes, the night-life of Golfe Juan and Juan-les-Pins, ceramics wherever you cast your eye in Picasso's Vallauris, and a visit to the glass-blowing workshop in Biot.

Next comes Cannes, the oasis of international high-society, an Eldorado for gourmets, with its festival atmosphere, yacht-mania and starlets. From here you can make an excursion out to the Lérins Islands, or follow the tracks of Napoleon through Mougins (with its renowned restaurants) to the centre of France's celebrated perfume industry at Grasse.

After Cannes, the uniquely beautiful landscape of the Corniche de L'Esterel begins: red cliffs of volcanic stone, indented capes and little bays, swimming beaches and yacht harbours. Located along this stretch is St Raphael, which was once described as a 'stately, old-fashioned Riviera town'; right next to it is Fréjus, on the Via Aurelia. Those interested in history should definitely not miss this 'Roman City' and the medieval cathedral quarter.

1. The *Grande Dame* of the Riviera

The Promenade des Anglais; a drink at the Hôtel Negresco, the town centre and luxury boutiques, the old town, the harbour, Cimiez, the Musée Chagall (allow a whole day).

Nikaia, Nice, Nissa-la-Bella or simply l'Olive, the *Grande Dame* of the Riviera, as it was known in its Golden Age, the era of crinolines, empresses (Eugénie) and queens (Victoria), has filled out somewhat since then. With a population of 400,000, the city has spread back from the sea over the surrounding hills, and west as far as the airport. The **Promenade des Anglais**, so-named because the English were responsible for its construction, follows the broad sweep of the Baie des Anges. Despite the heavy traffic which has replaced the pedestrians who once sauntered along in the shade of the palms, the Promenade has still managed to keep something of its original splendour.

'If you would like to see the most beautiful land in the world, here it is.' So wrote painter Pierre Auguste Renoir to Berthe Morisot, while simultaneously qualifying his praise: 'In winter, of course, it occurs to me that it's more like some kind of hot-house into which people with fragile health take refuge.' Here he is re-

ferring to a mistaken notion that the mild climate of the Côte would be therapeutic to people with lung complaints, an error which, well into the 19th century, misled many people into spending their winters here, or even settling permanently. More caustically, De Maupassant called it: '...a hospital of the *monde*, death's waiting room, the blooming graveyard of Europe's high nobility.'

It wasn't until the 20th century that Nice began to free itself from dependence on tourism. The airport – now the second busiest in France – was built in 1957, the university founded in 1965, and various colleges, convention centres, arts centres and museums have followed.

This itinerary begins at the western end of the Promenade des Anglais, stopping first at the **Musée International d'Art Naïf**, located on the Avenue Val Marie. It is the richest museum of its kind, with an inventory of some 6,000 paintings from 27 countries. The 300 works on permanent display, donated by the collector and art critic Jakovsky, are done full justice in the bright rooms of the castle.

The **Musée des Beaux Arts** at 33 Avenue des Baumettes is well worth a visit. Here the main theme is academic painting of the 19th century. Modern art is scarcely represented, with the exception of the Dufy Collection, which is exhibited on a rotating basis. Back on the Promenade, continue eastwards to the beautiful **Hôtel Negresco**, Nice's most famous landmark. Sitting on the terrace

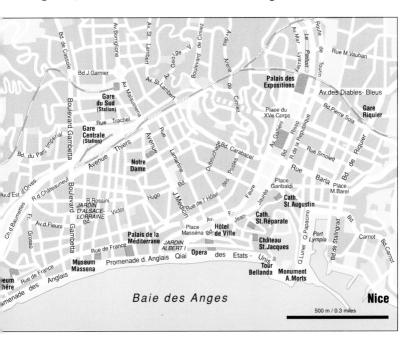

Nice is a city of frescos and painted tiles

with a drink or ice cream is an enjoyable way to admire the hotel's Belle Epoque architecture. Just behind the Negresco is the **Musée Masséna**, at 65 Rue de France, showing local history and the works of Bréa and Durandi, two of the earlier masters of Nice.

The **Palais de la Méditerranée**, built in 1929, is directly on the Promenade, although all that remains of it today is its splendid façade. A little further on is the **Jardin Albert I** with refreshing fountains and a huge permanent marquee which regularly stages rock concerts. This is the boarding-point for a mini-train which leaves every 20 minutes on a tour of the old town, the flower market and the castle gardens. The Turin-style **Place Masséna** represents the centre of the city these days, its fabulous fountains bordered by elegant red façades, a reminder that Nice is historically more Italian than French. This is the hub for luxury boutiques: designer names are on display in every window with prices to match. The **Avenue Jean Médecin** to the north of the square is the main shopping street, a wide thoroughfare shaded by plane trees. Here you will find the Galeries Lafayette, France's main department store, and Nice Etoile, a big shopping centre. Santazur at No. 11 gives information about half-day excursions which take place on Monday, Wednesday and Friday afternoons and include a tour of Nice and its various quarters, monuments, traditions and activities. The **Rue Masséna/Rue de France** is a pedestrian zone with busy terrace cafés and restaurants as well as shops.

Leaving modern Nice, head for the old town and the harbour, which are located on the other side of the Paillon River. The area around the river was the heart of the town's activity during the last century, but the river can no longer be seen. It has been bridged over by squares, avenues, and the **Acropolis** arts,

convention and exhibition centre which is anchored in the river-bed by five immense arches. Both the exterior and interior are decorated with the works of contemporary artists (Volti, Vasarely, Arman, César and others), which harmonise well with the architectural style. A new theatre and museum of modern art complete this important complex.

La Vieille Ville, called the *babazouk* in Niçois dialect, is the heart and soul of Nice. This is the authentic Nissa-la-Bella, a true delight for the senses. Here, the alleys are narrow and the houses tall; the façades are colourfully ornamented with flowers and laundry hung out to dry; the hubbub of southern lands is in evidence all day, mixed with loud voices and happy laughter.

From the Acropolis (from which you can walk all the way down to the sea through a series of gardens known as the **Promenade des Arts**), you should set off for the **Place Garibaldi,** which is surrounded by houses with loggias. The plaza is named in memory of the Italian nationalist Giuseppe Garibaldi (1807-82) who was born here. Nearby is the **Eglise St Martin-St Augustin**, the oldest parish church, in which Garibaldi was baptised and Luther celebrated mass. Across the street is a monument erected to Catherine Ségurane, who hitched her skirts up high and fought back the Turks with a knife in 1543.

The famous Nice fish-market takes place every morning (except Monday) on the **Place St François**. As you stroll around the old town, look up and admire the façades painted with frescoes and *trompe l'oeil*, the most famous of which can be seen as you drive down the **Quai des Etats-Unis** from east to west, and depicts a man on a ladder painting a palm tree on the wall.

Not so many years ago the old town was in a state of neglect; the municipality has recently stepped in with a major restoration project. One beneficiary is the **Place Rossetti**, around the **Cathédrale Ste Réparate**, where the façades have been repainted in magnificent hues of red, pink, ochre and yellow.

Nice's old town

The **Cours Saleya** lies between the old city and the sea. In the 19th century it was the meeting-place for high society; today it is a hive of activity from morning to night. Its famous flower market is open all day every day except Monday, when it gives way to an equally popular antiques and bric-à-brac market. Monday is the day to reserve a table for lunch at the **Safari**, specialising in local dishes, and observe the crowds from your ringside seat. The Cours Saleya is separated from the sea by the Ponchettes, once the wharf arsenal of the Savoyard-Sardinian navy, and from the rest of the old town by the **Préfecture**, formerly the palace of the Sardinian kings and, until recently, the

Cours Saleya flower market

official home of discredited mayor of Nice, Jacques Médecin.

From the Cours Saleya, head off up the 300-ft (90-m) hill between the old town and the harbour, known as the **Château** (even though it is nearly 300 years since a castle last stood there), which offers a fabulous panoramic view of the Baie des Anges and across the city. The city has thoughtfully provided several ways up: for those who climb the steps, there is a lift; or you can stroll up the winding path from the Rue Ségurane to the highest point. In the beautifully located cemetery which you pass on the way back down is the grave of the daughter of Consul Emil Jellinek. The name doesn't mean anything to you? Well, Jellinek won the Nice-Magnan car rally in 1899 in a Daimler, which he christened after his daughter Mercedes.

Crossing the Rue Ségurane, wander down to the harbour. Yachts and fishing-boats are moored here, as well as excursion ships and boats for rent. Car ferries to Corsica leave almost daily from the outer harbour. On the Quai des Deux Emmanuel is the famous, though not exactly cheap, gourmet spot **L'Esquinade**. Nearby, at 25 Boulevard Carnot, is the **Musée Terra Amata**, with exhibits proving that Nice was inhabited 400,000 years ago.

Cimiez (the Roman *Cemenelum*) can be best reached via the Boulevard de Cimiez, the route also taken by the coaches of the Belle Epoque when the guests of the Winter Palace and the Hotels Ermitage, Alhambra and Regina returned from the sea back up to their hill. In the 1st century BC, after the conquest of the Alpes Maritimes, which represented an important communication route to Gaul and Spain, the Romans constructed the Via Julia Augusta along the coast, and on the hills of Cimiez they erected their own town of *Cemenelum*, intended to rival the existing Greek town of Nikaia (Nice). It is interesting to see the splendid architecture of the Belle Epoque, as well as the recent excavations of Roman ruins, which include an amphitheatre, where one of the world's best jazz festivals takes place every July, and Roman baths which date from the 3rd century.

At the **Place du Monastère** is the entrance to the cemetery where painters Raoul Dufy (1877-1953) and Henri Matisse (1869-1954), and writer Martin du Gard are buried.

Cimiez is home to several museums: the **Musée d'Archéologie** at 160 Avenue des Arènes, the **Musée Chagall** (on the corner of Boulevard de Cimiez and Avenue Dr Ménard) (closed Tuesday during winter), which was designed to house Chagall's masterpiece *Messages Bibliques*, and the biggest single collection of his work.

The **Musée Matisse** (closed Tuesday during winter) in the Villa des Arènes has recently been completely renovated, and shows the development of this versatile artist with paintings, drawings, prints and bronze figures. Matisse lived in Nice for 20 years, at one time on the Cours Saleya, and latterly in the Hôtel Regina, which had been built for Queen Victoria in 1897.

Carneval (Carnival)

Carneval begins three weeks before Shrove Tuesday and is Nice's largest and most famous festival. The costumed parade was already established by 1848, when it often degenerated into a chalk and flour battle. In 1873, festival floats appeared for the first time and shortly thereafter came the figures and caricatures. The parades and flower battles which occur today and the burning of the King's float, accompanied by a big fireworks display, attract visitors from all over the world.

The **Festival des Cougourdons** in March is a big folk festival which takes place in the Garden of the Arena in Cimiez. The **Fêtes des Mais**, also held in Cimiez on the four Sundays of the month of May, are a delightful combination of evening dances, picnics on the green, and folklore presentations.

Restaurants

Inexpensive (Under 100FF)

AU SOLEIL
7 Rue d'Italie.
Tel: 93 88 77 74

LA MERANDA
4 Rue de la Terrane
Closed August (no telephone).

NISSA SOCCA
5 Rue St. Réparate
Tel: 93 80 18 35.

Moderate

LE SAFARI
1 Cours Saleya
Tel: 93 80 18 44

Expensive

LES DENTS DE LA MER
2 Rue St François de Paule
Tel: 93 80 99 16

L'ESQUINADE
5 Quai des Deux-Emmanuel
Tel: 93 89 59 36

LE CHANTECLER
37 Promenade des Anglais, in the
Hôtel Negresco.
Tel: 93 88 39 51

Accommodation

Inexpensive

HOTEL ALFA
30 Rue Masséna
Tel: 93 87 88 83

HOTEL LES ORANGERS
10 bis Avenue Durante
Tel: 93 87 51 41

NOUVEL HOTEL
19 Boulevard Victor Hugo
Tel: 93 87 15 00

RELAIS DE RIMIEZ
128 Avenue de Rimiez
Tel: 93 81 18 65

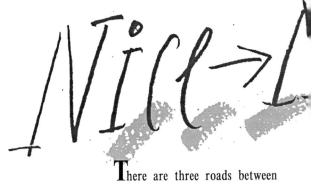

Nice → ...

There are three roads between Nice and Menton: the Basse Corniche follows the beautiful stretch of coast, but can be busy especially in summer, the Moyenne Corniche is the fastest, and the Grande Corniche is for nature-lovers and picnickers.

Basse Corniche

2. The Coastal Road (N98)

Villefranche: the medieval Rue Obscure, fish at La Mère Germaine; St Jean-Cap-Ferrat: the Billionaires' Peninsula, a walk around the cape; Beaulieu. (Nice-Menton 20 miles [31km]; with stops in Villefranche, Beaulieu and St Jean-Cap-Ferrat. Allow half a day).

'At this place between heaven and earth the world stands still.' So Maurice Maeterlinck, winner of the 1911 Nobel Prize for Literature,

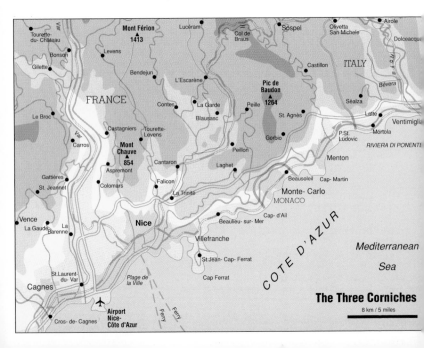

The Three Corniches

8 km / 5 miles

Villefranche

described the white and ochre palace with which he fell immediately in love, in his work *Les Sept Fées d'Orlamondé*. Today the **Palais Maeterlinck** is Nice's most recent exclusive hotel. Although the rooms are beyond the budget of most of us (from around £150 a night low season), the restaurant is open to the public and offers splendid views from Cap Ferrat to Cap d'Antibes. It is located just as you leave Nice on the Basse Corniche going towards Villefranche. (30 Boulevard Maeterlinck, tel: 92 00 72 00.)

Villefranche (Free City) is on one of the most beautiful inlets on the Mediterranean. Where the yachts and sporting boats drop

anchor today there was once a naval port in which galleys were constructed and in whose deep waters the Queen of France unexpectedly went swimming in 1538 when the gangplank to her ship collapsed. The tall, colourful façades of the old town line the attractive fishing harbour, which is one of the most pleasant settings in the region for a leisurely lunch. Several restaurants have terraces overlooking the water, but my favourite, and also that of Jean Cocteau, is **La Mère Germaine**, which serves excellent fish dishes.

The picturesque tangle of alleys and steps, and the arched 13th century **Rue Obscure** have barely changed since the Middle Ages.

On the keyside is the **Chapelle St Pierre** which was decorated

On Cap Ferrat

by Jean Cocteau in 1957, who grew up in Villefranche. The **Hôtel Welcome** in which he lived from time to time, still exists today and is thoroughly recommended.

The imposing **Citadel**, erected at the end of the 16th century for the protection of the bay, houses the **Goetz-Boumeester Museum**, primarily displaying abstract paintings as well as works of Picasso, Miró and Hartung. In the same complex is the **Volti Museum**, dedicated to native artists. It features sculptures of female figures displayed in the large courtyard of the citadel.

From the **Pont St Jean** you should take a drive round **Cap Ferrat**, sometimes known as the 'Billionaires' Peninsula'. The 6-mile (10 km) road takes you past high hedges and sturdy gates, behind which you catch glimpses of beautifully preserved villas set in well-tended parkland. Former residents include King Leopold II of Belgium, who chose the site because of its reputation for having the most pleasant climate in France. On his 35-acre (14 hectare) estate, Les Cèdres, he built a palace for himself and three villas for his mistresses. In 1926 Somerset Maugham bought the Villa Mauresque, which was built by the king's confessor Monsignor Charmeton. The gardens of Les Cèdres are open to the public; in addition to 15,000 rare plants set in fabulous lush woodland.

It is also possible to visit the former residence of the **Baroness Ephrussi de Rothschild**, which she had built to house her private art collection. The beautiful Italian-style palace now belongs to the state and is open as a museum, displaying mainly 18th-century Italian furniture, porcelain, carpets and paintings. Perhaps the most interesting part of the visit is the splendour of the villa itself and its wonderful grounds.

Edith Piaf also had a house on the Cap, the Villa Sospiro, as did David Niven and, more recently, the Rolling Stones and Tina Turner. It is thanks to these villas, often unoccupied and well-protected by dogs and heavily armed bodyguards, that the beauty and quiet of the peninsula has been preserved.

Local oysters

Among the most impressive residences are the Maryland, the Vigie, Mes Roches and Serena, all located on **Passable Beach**, a sandy beach which slopes gently down to the sea, and from which you can take a shady footpath leading round to the village of **St Jean-Cap Ferrat**. This thoroughfare is the former customs road, and along the way you will find small, uncrowded inlets, ideal for swimming. A splendid view rewards those with the courage to climb the 164 steps to the lighthouse, one of the most modern in France. At the tip of the peninsula is a tower which served as a jail in the 18th century.

St Jean itself is little more than a tiny harbour lined with a few cafés and old houses, and despite modernisation it has managed to retain its picturesque charm.

Beaulieu is among the warmest places on the French Riviera, a luxurious oasis of quiet refinement for the well-to-do. Somewhat more affordable is the mouth-watering seafood gratin served at the **African Queen** on the Yachting Harbour. The fish-stews and mini-*bouillabaisses* at the **Key Largo** are also worth travelling for. If you feel like a pleasant after-lunch stroll, the **Maurice Rouvier Promenade** leads around the Baie des Fourmis past luxurious villas to St Jean-Cap Ferrat. Alternatively, for the more energetic, the footpath to the **Plateau St Michel** is a steep climb up the escarpment affording beautiful views on the way. Allow a good hour and a half there and back. The **Villa Kerylos**, a reconstruction of an ancient Greek villa, is worth a visit.

Afterwards head for **Eze Bord-de-Mer**, from where it is possible

to climb up to **Eze** village on foot, as Nietzsche did while conceiving the third part of *Thus Spake Zarathustra*. This is one of the French Riviera's most attractive and dramatic hilltop villages (*see page 46*). Then, travelling by way of the **Cap d'Ail**, whose beautiful villas are secluded among fir trees and cypresses on the lower cliffs of the **Tête de Chien** (the shape of a dog's head), you will arrive at the **Principality of Monaco**.

Monaco

The Old City: the Cathedral, the Musée Océanographique, the plaza in front of the Prince's Palace; the Jardin Exotique; the Parc Paysager and the Rose Garden. Tips for Monte Carlo by day and by night. (Allow a day).

Descendents of the Grimaldi family are to be found in Cagnes, Beuil, Naples and Genoa. It was Francesco Grimaldi, driven out of Genoa, who took control of Monaco in 1297 in a coup in which he and his accomplices disguised themselves as monks. Although he was unable to hold Monaco, to this day the armed monk in the Grimaldi coat of arms stands as a reminder of the coup. In 1308 the Grimaldi family bought Monaco from the Genoese. The history of the Principality is fraught with family strife and occupation by

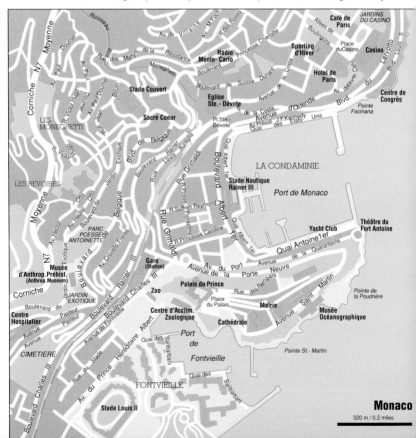

Monaco

320 m / 0.2 miles

Monaco, home to the rich and famous

various powers, such as the Spanish, the French and the Sardinians.

In 1861 Roquebrune and Menton, until then part of the state, were incorporated into France, leaving Monaco much smaller and considerably poorer. In an attempt to attract aristocratic tourism, Prince Charles III decided to turn Monaco into a health and leisure resort and to allow gambling, which was forbidden in the neighbouring countries. He eliminated direct taxation and created Monte Carlo, where, in 1862, he had a small casino constructed. Although this was not immediately successful in overcoming his financial problems, the situation changed when François Blanc bought the Casino and, with several associates, founded the **Société des Bains de Mer** (SBM). Before long a new city came into existence around the Casino, with palatial hotels, villas and magnificent grounds. Towards the end of the 19th century the rich guests finally appeared, although only in winter at first.

Today there are several million visitors a year. In the 1950s, soon after Prince Rainier III came to power, Aristotle Onassis was the controlling shareholder of SBM. If he had had his way, he would have restricted Monaco as the exclusive enclave of the super-rich, whereas Rainier wanted to open it up to ordinary tourists. Rainier won and, under the influence of Princess Grace, adopted an American style of marketing. In the meantime the SBM has grown into a gigantic enterprise, whose restaurants have amassed a total of five Michelin stars. Three of these stars were won by chef Alain Ducasse of the Louis XV in the **Hôtel de Paris**; his former apprentice Caironi has been awarded one for the Grill, also in the Hôtel de Paris; with the fifth going to Garnier at La Coupole in the **Hôtel Mirabeau**.

The Principality is now an exclusive tax-paradise for a privileged few: indeed, the Prince on average grants fewer than 300 applications for citizenship every year. Boris Becker, Alain Prost and Bjorn

Eldorado for boat fans

Borg are among the lucky ones. The British writer Anthony Burgess punched the keys of his much-loved old Remington typewriter here up until his death in 1994. He took refuge in Monaco after the Mafia threatened to kidnap his son.

It is one of the Principality's attractions that its 30,000 inhabitants (of whom scarcely more than 4,000 are genuine Monégasques) live in total security. The video observation system is as discreet as it is effective, and it is one of the most efficient in the world. Fifty cameras observe the city's 'vulnerable' points day and night. In addition there are 400 police officers (reputed to be the most handsome police force in the world) with modern equipment, supported by a further 200 civilian security officers. In Monaco there is certainly no danger in displaying your wealth, a fact attested by the number of luxury yachts, expensive automobiles, haute-couture clothing and precious jewellery.

The tiny Princely State includes the old city on the Rock, Monte Carlo, La Condamine which is the harbour and business district situated between the two, and the new town of Fontvieille, built on reclaimed land and devoted mostly to business and an impressive sports stadium which was opened in 1985.

This itinerary begins in Monaco, the capital of this miniature state, which is built on the 1,000-ft (300-m) wide and 2,600-ft (800-m) long cliff, known as the Rock, that extends out to sea. In the **Cathedral** there are several altar paintings by Louis Bréa. Princess Grace is buried nearby. In the alleyways of the Old City you can often hear Les Petits Chanteurs de Monaco on Sunday mornings as they sing mass in the Cathedral. The **Placette Bosio** commemorates the poet Guillaume Apollinaire, who used to walk through the shady alleys of the **Jardin St Martin**. The members of the Grimaldi dynasty are immortalised as waxwork figures in the **Musée de Cire**, which is located on the Rue Basse, one of the most picturesque steets in the old quarter.

The Place du Casino

It is not difficult to see why it took eleven years to build the **Musée Oceanographic**. It was founded in 1910 by Prince Albert I, whose passion for research took him on many sea voyages. The aquarium has more than 90 tanks. Nearby you can find out about the history of the town in the **Musée du Vieux Monaco**. Continue to the **Place du Palais** in front of the Prince's Palace, which, with its cannons and cannonballs, has something of an operatic air. An impression which is strengthened by the changing of the guard (every day at 11.55am). From the parapet on one side of the square there is a fabulous view of the harbour, of Monte Carlo, of the coast along to the point of Bordighera, of the new quarter of Fontvieille and of the Cap d'Ail. In summer it is possible to visit part of the Prince's Palace; the **Napoleonic Museum** in one of the wings is open all year round.

Leaving the Rock by bus, the next stop is the **Jardin Exotique**, an amazing feat of gardening on a cliff. The 8,000 species of

View of two harbours

plants include varieties of cactus from South America, Mexico and Africa. Another green oasis of peace amid all the skyscrapers is the **Parc Paysager** with its freshwater lake, and the **Rose Garden**, created by Prince Rainier in memory of Princess Grace.

You should then move on to the exclusive, exotic, extravagant world of **Monte Carlo** and the **Place du Casino**, with its immaculate gardens surrounded by the Casino itself flanked on one side by the Hôtel de Paris and on the other by the more recent **Café de Paris**. Lunch at the Café de Paris is definitely *the* thing to do, although, prices being what one would expect in Monte Carlo, you could just make do with a coffee, before strolling next-door for a look at the Casino, well worth a visit for its extravagant architecture and decoration. The slot machines are open all day and admission is free, but to really get a feel of the atmosphere you should go into the **Salons Privés** (open from late afternoon). Should you decide to try your luck at the roulette tables, you should hope for better fortune than the 19th century courtesan La Belle Otéro, who lost everything in a single evening (although she then went on to win back a fortune by gambling the gold buttons on her dress).

Seeing – and being seen – outside the Café de Paris

The **Salle Garnier**, straight ahead as you enter the Casino, is the wonderfully elaborate setting for opera, theatre, ballet and concerts, complete with theatre boxes for royalty. Should you have the opportunity to attend a gala performance, admiring the outfits and diamonds of the high society is entertainment in itself.

Venturing back out of the Casino, shoppers should head for the **Rue Grimaldi** or the **Galérie Metropole**, beneath Monte Carlo's deluxe hotel the **Metropole Palace**. Alternatively, the **Musée des Automates** on the **Avenue Princesse Grace** right down by the beach houses an interesting collection of 18th and 19th-century dolls and automata, which are set in motion several times a day. No visit to visit Monte Carlo would be complete without a stop at the Häagen Dazs outdoor ice-cream parlour, Place du Casino.

The choice of fine restaurants for dinner is endless. My favourite for Italian specialities is **Rampoldi's** (Avenue des Spélugues, tel: 93 30 70 65); another is **Polpetta** (Rue Roqueville, tel: 93 50 67 84), or for a real splash you could always dine in style at the Louis XV in the Hotel de Paris.

Entertainment is also plentiful; for bars with atmosphere try the **Snooker Pub** on Rue Langle, tel: 93 25 08 34, or the English haunt **Flashman's**, tel: 93 30 09 03. The Casino and the **Hôtel Loews** both have cabarets, and the **Monte Carlo Sporting Club** puts on star-studded shows in summer. To dance the night away, your best chances of keeping company with the jet-set are at **Jimmy'z**, **Parady'z** or the **Livingroom**.

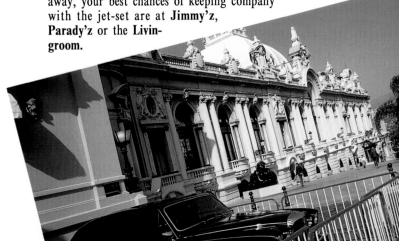

Special events

January: Monte Carlo Rally.
February: International TV Festival.
April: Monte Carlo Tennis Open.
May: Formula 1 Grand Prix.
June: Monte Carlo Golf Open.
July/August: Concert in the Palace courtyard; Fireworks Festival.
19 November: Monaco's National Holiday.
December: Circus festival.

Restaurants

Inexpensive

LE ST PIERRE
Rue de la Turbie. Tel: 93 30 99 96.
LA STREGA
Rue de la Colle. Tel: 93 30 16 30.
BACCUS
Rue de la Turbie. Tel: 93 30 19 35.

Moderate

RAMPOLDI'S
Avenue des Spélugues. Tel: 93307065.
POLPETTA
Rue Roqueville. Tel: 93 50 67 84.

Expensive

HOTEL DE PARIS
Tel: 92 16 30 00.
Le Louis XV. Closed Tuesday and Wednesday, except July and August. Closed December and 2 weeks February/March. Complete menus 700FF; à la carte 800FF.
Le Grill. Complete menu 300FF; à la carte 500FF.

HOTEL HERMITAGE
La Belle Epoque. Tel: 92 16 40 00. Complete menu 300FF, à la carte 500FF.
Terrasse de la Belle Epoque. Open July–August.

HOTEL MIRABEAU
Tel: 93 50 80 80/93 50 80 93
La Coupole. Closed lunchtime July–August. Complete menus 250–400FF; à la carte 400FF.

MONTE CARLO BEACH HOTEL
Tel: 93 28 66 66.
La Potinière. Around the swimming-pool. Summer only. 400-500FF.
Le Rivage. A la carte.
La Vigie. July/August. Buffet 230FF.

VISTA PALACE HOTEL
Tel: 92 10 40 00.
Le Vistaero. Around 450FF.

CAFÉ DE PARIS
Tel: 93 50 57 75.
All year, 8am–5am. From 200FF.

MONTE CARLO CASINO
Tel: 92 16 22 11.
Le Train Bleu. A la carte.
Le Privé. Open mid September–June. A la carte.
Le Cabaret. Open mid September–June. From 380FF.

ROGER VERGÉ CAFÉ
Tel: 05 11 12 01.
Closed Sunday. Menus 90-110FF.

MONTE CARLO SPORTING CLUB
Salles des étoiles. Tel: 92 16 22 44. Dining, show and dancing from the end of June–mid-September.
Maona Fuji. Tel: 93 50 05 45. Dinner from end of June–mid-September. Japanese cuisine. Complete menu 400FF. In winter the restaurant moves to Galérie Métropole.
Maona Exotique. Tel: 92 16 22 55. June–mid-September. Chinese and exotic dishes. Complete menu 320FF.

Affordable Accommodation

HOTEL DE FRANCE
Tel: 93 30 24 64.
Next to the train station.
HOTEL BOERI
Tel: 93 78 38 10.
29 Avenue Général Leclerc, Beausoleil.
HOTEL TERMINUS
Tel: 93 30 20 70.
9 Avenue Prince-Pierre.

4. The Lemon Capital

The pedestrian zone Rue St Michel; Palais Carnolès; gardens including the view from the Jardin des Colombières; excursions from Menton, which is also a cultural centre. (Allow half a day for Menton, a whole day with excursions.)

The harbour at Menton

With 300 days of sunshine per year and a backdrop of protective mountains which are covered in citrus and olive groves, Menton has one of the warmest climates on the Riviera. It also has a casino, nightclubs, yacht harbours and endless sandy beaches.

Determined to make the most of the climate, the city's maxim is to offer its citizens and visitors an impressive array of cultural events: concerts, museums, exhibitions, a theatre season from November to April, the Lemon Festival in February, flower festivals in summer with magnificent parades, festive evenings in the **Parc du Pian**, a circle of poets and the Katherine Mansfield Prize, awarded for the best novel (the New Zealand-born author spent some time in Menton around the turn of the century).

The well-known Chamber Music Festival, created by the Hungarian André Borocz some 45 years ago, is especially worthy of mention. Borocz's hatred of ants drove him to despair on his holiday in Juan-les-Pins, moving him to take quarters with friends in Menton. Here, on a beautiful August evening, he discovered the Italianate plaza in front of the **Eglise St Michel**; the sound of Haifitz playing a Bach violin concerto drifted out of an open window and created an acoustic backdrop for the sunset. Borocz was moved by this serendipitous weaving of events, and sought to reproduce the experience for others. The intimate *parvi* provides a unique setting for the chamber music festival performances: the ochre of the largest and most beautiful Baroque church in the area, the rose hue of the adjacent chapel, grey and white cobblestones arranged into the Grimaldi coat of arms... and a ceiling of glowing stars.

Not far from the Eglise St Michel is the **Town Hall** where the room used to conduct marriage ceremonies is decorated by Jean Cocteau. If you stroll down towards the harbour, you will come to the **Musée Cocteau** in the little 17th-century fort. Behind the church of St Michael, the Rue Longue follows the Via Julia Augusta, the former main traffic artery and a route originally laid by the Romans. The **Rue St Michel** with its little orange trees is a popular pedestrian shopping zone; below it is the charming **Place aux Herbes**, and nearby, the covered market, next to the **Place du Marché** with its flower stalls.

At the west end of the town is the 18th-century **Palais Carnolès**, the former summer residence of the Monaco royal family. This attractive pink and white palace is set in a beautiful park and looks very Italian; its abundant art collection is well worth a visit.

Menton is famous for its many gardens. The **Jardin Biovès** was built right over the Careï River. With its tall palms, citrus trees, fountains and statues, the garden is the centre of February's Lemon Festival.

Up above the church the old cemetery affords some of the best views of town and sea. The artist Aubrey Beardsley is among its illustrious residents. Another beautiful view over the rising arcades of Old Menton with its tall, narrow houses framed by the mountain backdrop, is to be enjoyed from among the pines and cypresses of the **Jardin des Colombières** (Rue Ferdinand Bac), gardens which were laid out by the author and architect Ferdinand Bac. The **Jardin Botanique** contains some 700 species of Mediterranean and tropical flora.

There are numerous possible outings to be made from Menton. You might venture out to **Gorbio** (D23) or **St Agnès** (D22), two attractive mountain villages with wonderful views of the coast. Or you may choose to take the D2566 to the **Annonciade Monastery**, which has been a destination for pilgrims since the 11th century. There is also the Forest of Menton, a pleasant place for hiking, up towards **Sospel** beyond the **Col de Castillon**. On Fridays (market-day) you may like to visit the Italian town of **Venimiglia** just over the border.

Menton

320 m / 0.2 miles

Eze

5. Pleasures of the Palate

Eze Village; the ruins of the Saracen fortress with a view over the entire Riviera; dining in the Château Eza or in the Chèvre d'Or; the exclusive residential area of Cap Martin on the Peninsula (Nice–Menton 20 miles [31km]; half a day).

The broad and much-improved N7 is the fastest route from Nice to **Eze Village**. To get up into the village, join the throng passing through the gate of the old Saracen fortress on the Avenue du Jardin Exotique and on up the Rue du Brec to the church with its Baroque interior. Then follow the Rue de la Paix and the Rue du Château with its dark archways, and climb the steps to the **Jardin Exotique** at the highest point of the steep hill. There is little left of the castle, destroyed on the orders of Louis XIV, but standing at this point you are 1,407ft (429m) above sea-level and with a sweeping panorama across the entire Riviera. On the way back down stop to admire the 14th-century **Chapelle des Pénitents Blancs**, a simple building whose outside walls are decorated with enamel paintings.

At the end of the Rue de la Pise you will see the Moorish gateway on your right, and on your left the former residence of Prince William of Sweden. Now a charming hotel and restaurant, the **Château Eza** (tel: 93 41 12 24) will satisfy the most demanding of clientele. The **Chèvre d'Or** (tel: 93 41 12 12) is a second gourmet temple in the Rue du Barri. You should definitely stop for lunch in one of these two restaurants, but be sure to reserve a table. Dining here cannot be described as inexpensive but it is certainly a unique experience.

Past Eze, the Moyenne Corniche continues around the Tête de Chien and then passes above the Principality of Monaco (see *Monaco Itinerary, page 38*). Remaining on the same road, you will arrive in **Beausoleil**, which nestles in the south cliffs of the Mont des Mules. After that the Corniche leads on past the Vista Palace Hotel and joins the coastal road just east of **Roquebrune**, a town which is divided into two parts: a modern seaside resort and an old village (see *Grande Corniche Itinerary, page 49*).

Continuing east, you will come to **Cap Martin,** Menton's most exclusive neighbourhood. This peninsula is lush with olive groves, cypresses, mimosas and pine woods, among which are splendid hidden villas and grounds, whose owners are no doubt very happy that there is nothing else in this area to attract tourists. The mild climate and flourishing vegetation have long appealed to those with the means of living here: the beautiful Sissi of Austria loved the south and the sea; the French Empress Eugénie hoped for an improvement in her illness while staying here; King Umberto of Italy, Sir Winston Churchill, Le Corbusier and the Chanels came here for the peace and quiet.

The 'immortal' Greta Garbo, always on the run from the public eye, hid here in the splendidly located estate of the Russian Princess Anna Chervachidzé, which today belongs to the Lebanese billionaire Hani Salaam. Silvano Mangano and the Italian film producer Dino de Laurentiis have frequently tarried here in the residence Casa del Mare. So be on the lookout – although of course recognising celebrities in the flesh is not always easy.

The Cannes coast

6. Via Julia Augusta

From Nice to Roquebrune via the Grande Corniche: the Ferme St Michel; splendid mountain views; La Turbie and the Trophée des Alpes; Roquebrune village. (Allow half a day.)

Napoleon ordered the construction of this uppermost Corniche, which partly follows the course of the Roman Aurelian Way. As you leave Nice you pass the **Observatory** (Tel: 92 00 30 11) which was designed by Charles Garnier and Gustave Eiffel. It is open to the public on the second and fourth Saturdays of the month at 3pm, by appointment.

On this relatively quiet road you can comfortably turn your attention to the splendid landscape. Shortly before the **Col des 4-Chemins** you come to the entrance to the **Paillon Valley**, and through the opening you can see straight up to the Alps. Just past here, the **Ferme St Michel** (tel: 93 76 68 38, open evenings and Sunday only) offers a complete menu in a delightful setting. Though expensive, the price includes everything from the aperitif to the digestif.

Alternatively, as you pass the **Col d'Eze** a little further on, just

48

In the quiet hills

by the Hotel Hermitage, is the Plateau de la Justice, which is a lovely place for a picnic. From the Col d'Eze, at an altitude of 1,665ft (508m), there is an extensive view north towards the upper Var and Vésubie valleys, and a hiking path which leads into the **Parc de la Revere**, where you can study Mediterranean vegetation in detail.

The **Trophée des Alpes (Alpine Trophy)** is a restored Roman victory monument, visible from a considerable distance, which nowadays houses an ornithological station, which stages flight demonstrations by birds of prey. The Trophy originally gave the nearby settlement its name: Tropea Augusti – which later became **La Turbie**. The Rue Comte de Cessole, formerly the Via Julia, leads past medieval houses up to the monument. Despite a mention in the poetry of Dante, and the honour of an overnight stop by Napoleon, the village still has a pleasantly unassuming charm.

The road continues down to **Roquebrune**, France's only preserved settlement dating from the Carolingian period (the Frankish dynasty of Charlemagne, AD742–814).The name of the labyrinthine little village comes from the reddish-brown cliffs into which it was built. Stroll through the steep covered streets and climb the ancient staircases up to the 13th-century keep, which served both for defence and as a residence. Its interior bears witness to the modest living conditions of the feudal lord.

For over 500 years a procession has been held in Roquebrune on the afternoon of 5 August to commemorate one held by the locals in 1467, which is said to have prevented an epidemic of the plague. Today the streets are festively decorated and illuminated with thousands of flickering oil lanterns. Two hundred metres past the village on the Menton road there is a 1,000-year-old olive tree, believed to be one of the oldest in the world.

Nice → Ven

7. Renoir and his Olive Groves

The yacht harbour of St Laurent; La Gaude; Haut-de-Cagnes and the castle. (14 miles/22 km. Allow a good half day.)

Leave Nice on the Promenade des Anglais, the six-lane coastal road heading west.

Until 1860, when the County of Nice fell to France, the River Var represented the border between France and the Kingdom of Sardinia. The town of **St Laurent-du-Var** was in charge of the river crossing. Travellers from Paris to Nice, who had spent 12 uncomfortable days in their coaches, were carried on the shoulders of two strong men over the ford of the torrential mountain river. Today the crossing is much easier with three major roads crossing the now somewhat tamer river.

Just across the river from the airport is the imposing shopping centre **Cap 3000**. It has countless boutiques selling everything from designer names to the French mail-order house La Redoute, a wonderful modern supermarket, a Nouvelles Galeries department store, and an enormous free car park.

St Laurent yachting harbour is a pleasant place for a stroll, with a wide choice of restaurants should it be getting on for mealtime. **Sant'ana** (Tel: 93 07 02 24) is good for seafood.

If you are ready to get away from the hubbub of the coast, a good evasive move is to take the Corniche du Var (D118). This

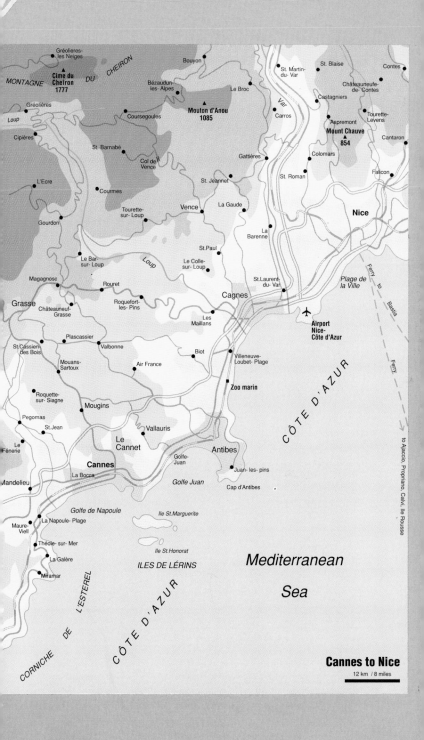

Cannes to Nice

12 km / 8 miles

Looking west from Nice

road, which provides beautiful views of the hinterlands of Nice, leads past the IBM Research Centre to **La Gaude** (turn left on to the D18) where the writer Marcel Pagnol spent some time. This former wine-makers' village is home to a 'living museum' of local flora and fauna: **La Coupole** (Quarter Ste Appolonie, tel: 93 24 97 47; open every day 2–6pm except Monday), was founded by the Danish sculptor Ib Schmedes, who has lived in La Gaude for over 40 years.

Now you have a pleasant choice: from La Gaude you can either drive on to **St Jeannet**, passing along the way a 14th-century castle originally owned by the Knights Templar (and today, after years of renovation, occupied by the appropriately-named French actress Viviane Romance), and then on to **Vence**, (see *Vence* and *Around Vence* itineraries, *pages 56 and 60*), or you can continue down to the coast via the hill-top village of **Haut-de-Cagnes**, which is well worth a side-trip of itself.

If you decide in favour of the latter, as you come down into the

Haut-de-Cagnes

Musée de l'Olivier

town of Cagnes-sur-Mer, follow signs right to the Haut-de-Cagnes. The best places to park are either in the underground multi-storey garage built into the mountain, where your car is taken down by lift, or anywhere you can find room on the street on your way up to the castle. The only way to see the old village is on foot; every corner hides attractive houses, tiny flower-filled squares, alleyways and arched passages.

The medieval castle was originally a fortress built by Rainier Grimaldi, Lord of Monaco and Admiral of France, in 1309. One year later Grimaldi had a citadel built there as a symbol of his powerful family. The *Cagnois* who sheltered within its walls cultivated wheat, wine and olives on the neighbouring hills. These staples, as well as fish from the harbour of Cros de Cagnes, were brought up into the village on mules.

In the 17th century Henri Grimaldi had the 300-year-old citadel remodelled into a magnificently appointed castle. With the coming of the French Revolution this feudal life came to an abrupt end, ending an era of considerable luxury. Gaspard Grimaldi was forced

Inside the Grimaldi citadel

to leave Cagnes and abandon his castle along with it. He fled to Nice, a duchy which in those days still belonged to the counts of Savoy.

St Peter's Church, located beneath the Porte de Nice, is equipped with an attractive wrought-iron bell tower of the sort commonly seen in Provence. The tombs of the Grimaldis of Cagnes are also located in this church.

The Château remained unoccupied until a buyer was finally found in the 19th century. It has belonged to the city of Cagnes-sur-Mer since 1939. Today the Castle-Museum houses the **Musée de l'Olivier Ethnographie**, where you can learn everything there is to know about the olive; the **Musée d'Art Moderne Méditerranéen** and the **Suzy Solidor Foundation**. The latter is especially interesting; it displays portraits of Suzy, a 1930s Parisian nightclub singer, by some 40 significant 20th-century artists.

Haut-de-Cagnes has always been of great significance for modern

Cagnes' Town Hall, once home to Renoir

painting: a number of German artists worked here in the 1930s, and since 1969 the castle has hosted the annual **Festival International de la Peinture** (30 June–30 September). For a more complete list of Côte d'Azur festivals and events, please consult the Calendar of Special Events on pages 108–9 of this book.

Auguste Renoir (1841–1919) is without doubt Cagnes' most famous painter. Towards the end of the last century, suffering from a painful attack of gout, the artist came to the South of France on the advice of his doctor. In Cagnes he found what he sought: a hilly, idyllic landscape, a favourable microclimate and, above all, wonderful light. It was always the light that fascinated Renoir, along with his friends Monet and Sisley. He worked in the open air, concentrating on the challenge of portraying sunlight and its reflections on canvas.

In 1903 he established himself in the Maison de la Poste, today the town hall. In 1907, he acquired, on the advice of his friend

Renoir's studio

who later became mayor of Cagnes, **Les Collettes**, a sizeable plot of land with very old olive trees. Here he built the house in which he spent the last 12 years of his life. In 1960 the city of Cagnes purchased the villa and installed the **Renoir Museum**. Since everything was left in its original condition, the visitor feels transported back to the time when Renoir, in great pain, had to be lifted out of his bed into his wheelchair and pushed out into the garden. There he spent hours before the easel in the shade of his beloved olive trees. There are also works by Bonnard and Dufy.

You can dine very well in **Des Peintres** (71 Montée de la Bourgade, tel: 93 20 83 08) almost the only address where you can sample such delectable crayfish. **Josy Jo** (tel: 93 20 68 76) is equally to be recommended. There the staff will not only explain all about the different kinds of figs, but they also prepare a delightfully tender piece of liver.

From Cagnes it is only a short distance to Vence, the next major destination in this book.

8. City of Artists

In and around the medieval hilltop town of Vence; Place du Peyra, the Forum of the old Roman town; the old town and Cathedral; Provençal cuisine in the Auberge des Seigneurs. (Nice 14 miles/22km; Antibes 12 miles/19km; Cannes 25 miles/39km; allow half a day.)

Typically Provençal: Vence

Vence is only 6 miles (10km) away from the sea, and yet you get the feeling here that you are in a completely different world. The locals proudly boast: 'Provence begins in Vence', and Mistral, the famous poet of this region, wrote in dialect: *'Desempiei Arle jusquá Venco — Escoutas me Gént de Prouvenco,'* which roughly translates as, 'From Arles to Vence the people speak Provençal'.

Those who have seen Chagall's painting *The Lovers of Vence* will be shocked at the first approaches, since the modern Vence outside the city walls with its horrible new buildings in no way resembles the *village perché* in the work of this poetic artist (for many centuries the farmers erected such settlements like eagles' nests at daring heights and put up fortification walls for security). However, the picturesque old Vence at the foot of the Baous mountains, which protect it from the cold north winds, has remained unchanged, having preserved its typically Provençal character especially well.

The medieval core of the city, surrounded by an elliptical wall with five gates, makes it rather difficult for the visitor to imagine the Roman city of Vintium. In those days Vence was already a popular health-resort because of its mild climate, and the water from the **Source de la Foux** was just as popular for its health benefits then as now.

Entering the city through the **Porte Peyra** you come to the **Place du Peyra**, the Forum of the old Roman city. The beautiful urn-shaped fountain here dates from 1822. Continue along the **Rue du Marché**, a colourful narrow market street, selling meat, fish, cheese, wine, fresh pasta, fruit and vegetables, to arrive at the **Place Clemenceau** on your left. The Town Hall is located here on the site of the former bishop's palace.

In 374, shortly after its conversion by the monks of St Honorat, Vence became an episcopal city, starting quite a tradition of venerable clerics. The bishops St Véran (5th century) and St Lambert (12th century) were declared saints; Farnese (16th century) declined the Vence bishop's crosier, going instead to the Holy See to become Pope Paul III. He proved to be quite generous to Vence, however, and donated several reliquaries.

Bishop Godeau was an enthusiastic visitor to the Hôtel des Rambouillet, which was then a centre of literary life, and he was made the first member of the Académie Française by Richelieu. Bishop Surian (18th century) parted with his fortune for the benefit of a hospital.

Vence's loss of rank as a bishop's see in 1801 can be traced to Napoleon and the Pope. At first the honour passed to Fréjus, then, in 1860, it went to the diocese of Nice when the right bank of the Var became permanently French.

On the site of the **Cathedral** there once stood a temple to Mars, followed by a Merovingian church. As a result of the repeated alteration and expansion of the original Roman building, the present structure is a peculiar mixture of styles. Inside are the tombs of saints Véran and Lambert, a mosaic by Chagall in the Baptistry, and a choir pew made of oak and pear-tree wood which was designed by Jacques Bellot of Grasse in the 15th century. Despite the five years of work that went into making the pew, it is evident from the detail that he did not lose his sense of humour.

From the Place Godeau, with a granite Roman column in the centre, you have a good view of the rectangular tower, a Renaissance door from 1575,

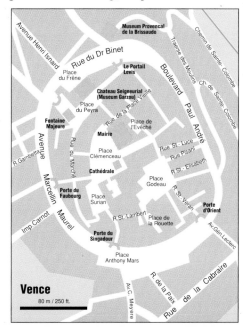

Vence

80 m / 250 ft.

courtyards and alleyways as well as a picturesque corner by the name of L'Enfer (Hell).

Continue along the Rue St Lambert and the Rue de l'Hotel de Ville to reach the **Porte du Singadour**. Directly opposite is a 15th-century fountain. If you turn left you pass the **Porte de l'Orient**, for which you once needed to have your own key. The date recorded up on the left of the gate commemorates the unsuccessful siege of the city by the Huguenots. The old Alphonse Toreille Seminary, constructed by Godeau in 1669, is located a short walking distance from here. The **Boulevard Paul André** leads along the city wall, large sections of which are still preserved. The view of the Baous and the outer spurs of the Alps is beautiful here.

Now return to the **Place du Peyra** by way of the **Portail Lévis** and the **Rue du Portail Lévis**. The Château Seigneurail built by Villeneuve in the 16th century is located on the **Place du Frêne**. Today it houses the **Musée Carzou**. The painter Carzou, who has small ironic blue eyes, a high forehead and white hair, bought an old *mas* (a southern French farmhouse) in Vence in 1958, because here he found the quiet, the relaxation and the freedom of spirit he needed for his creativity. The paintings, watercolours, drawings, sculpture and books exhibited in the château were donated to the museum by Carzou himself. Recently he has been working on the design of a chapel in Manosque.

The old **ash tree** on the plaza in front of the château is supposed to have been planted in the 16th century, in honour of Franz I and Pope Paul III. The restaurant **Auberge des Seigneurs** serves Provençal dishes in a dining room with a large, beautiful fireplace. According to — probably scurrilous — rumour, the restaurant is supposed to have lost its star because clandestine visiting representatives from the Michelin guides were served a dessert in the shape of a penis (tel: 93 58 04 24).

Many artists were attracted to Vence after World War I. Among

Spoiled for choice

others, André Gide, Paul Valéry, Chaim Soutine and Raoul Dufy made extended visits. In 1955, when the city had no more than 6,000 inhabitants, a new generation of artists came to Vence: Céline, Tzara, and Cocteau; Matisse, Chagall, Carzou and Dubuffet. Today Vence has a population of 15,000, and its artistic tradition still continues.

Arman, born in Nice, has been an American citizen since 1972, but every year he leaves New York to return to Vence. His house, which originally looked like an overturned, half-buried boat, now rather resembles a work of art. The wing added in 1980 is ornamented with 2,300 wash-tubs.

The artist Nall originally set himself up in Dubuffet's former studio. Dali, of whom he thought very highly, is supposed to have said to him: 'If you can succeed in portraying hair in such a way that you are convinced you can see it growing, then you can really paint.' He has now moved and created the NALL Foundation, where he provides a place for young artists to work.

Behind the Cathedral Georges Martin has a business which he has been operating alone for over 30 years. If you are looking for old wooden doors, closets, communion tables, window bars, fireplace grilles or wrought iron gates, then you should arrange a visit (Tel: 93 58 11 47).

Vence is not just an attractive vacation town, it's also a good starting point for excursions into the splendid hinterlands. I would be more than happy to provide lodging in my restored farm near here to individualists, art fans or those in need of relaxation who would like to get to know a bit of the real Provence (by previous arrangement only; 659 Chemin de la Gaude; Tel: 93 58 74 87). The first time you call you'll be picked up, since the route is complicated to describe.

You can enjoy very good Provençal cuisine in the **Farigoule** (Tel: 93 58 01 27) at 15 Rue Jean Isnard. The proprietress is sometimes quite severe; you should definitely make reservations. You can also sit outside in the **La Closerie des Genêts** (Tel: 93 58 33 25). The food is very good, although the service is variable.

9. Peaceful Mountain Villages

The Rosary Chapel by Matisse; the Baous; lunch at the Auberge St Jeannet; the mountain villages of Gattières and Le Broc; horse-riding at Ranch El Bronco; the Col de Vence (38 miles/60 km. Allow a whole day to do everything).

Vence viaduct

As you leave Vence heading north-east towards St Jeannet on the D2210, you have to watch carefully to avoid driving straight past the Provençal building with a glazed cross on its roof. Matisse was 80 when he designed and decorated the **Chapelle du Rosaire** (1947–51). It's certainly worth a visit, although this is only possible on Tuesdays and Thursdays (information available from the Vence Syndicat d'Initiative, Tel: 93 58 07 38).

Setting off again on the same road, you should pull over into the first lay-by to look back at the fully intact city wall surrounding Vence. As you do so, you will also discover a viaduct, a vestige of the 'good old days' when you could ride on the single track railway from Nice to Draguignan. The tunnels for this railway line, destroyed by the Resistance during World War II, serve today for cultivating very tasty mushrooms. Up to now this gastronomically important fact has prevented the train from being put back into service as a tourist attraction.

Continuing your drive you can already make out the imposing south face of the **Baou of St Jeannet**. Shortly before you leave the D2210 at the roundabout to turn left onto the cul-de-sac leading up to St Jeannet, souvenir-hunters have the chance to buy bizarrely formed hollowed-out gourds, some of which are also hand-painted by the daughter of this flourishing family enterprise.

Mountaineers come from all over the world to climb the sheer rock-face of the Baou of St Jeannet. Towering 1,300ft (400m) above

St Jeannet

the village, it has some 35 different possible ascents. With suitable shoes it is not difficult to hike to the summit, from which there is a spectacular panoramac view; allow an hour each way to do it comfortably.

After all this exercise you should be ready for a good lunch at the **Auberge de St Jeannet** (tel: 93 24 90 06), accompanied by a bottle of wine from the small local vineyard. Antoine's specialities include cold smoked breast of duck served on fresh young spinach glazed with hazelnut oil, ravioli in basil sauce, duck fillet with a hint of wild mountain honey, and lamb in a mild garlic sauce. The walls are hung with the works of contemporary artists (including some of my own), which are available for sale. The beautiful view down to the coast has inspired many an artist, such as Dunoyer de Segonzac, Carzou, Chagall and Poussin.

St Jeannet is one of the few villages withing easy striking distance of the coast to have retained its authenticity; here the tourists tend to be climbers and hikers and you will find local *épiceries* and *boulangeries* rather than arts and crafts workshops.

The next stop is the village of **Gattières**, a maze of picturesque alleyways offering wonderful views of the Alps. It is hard to imagine that winter sports are available for much of the year on the snow-capped peaks little more than an hour's drive away, in the resorts of Isola 2000, Auron and Valberg.

You should now branch off the D2210 onto the D2209, which follows the River Var, to the old village of **Carros**. Its attractive houses are marshalled around a castle on the top of a hill; a little below them, next to an old mill, there is a observation platform with a panoramic view. The 'new' Carros stretched below may be the pride of the community, but it disfigures the area with its

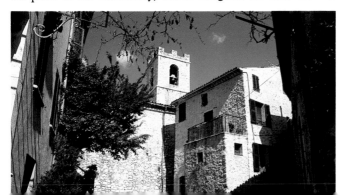

Carros

obtrusive new buildings. From here on the villages become smaller, quieter and more untouched.

Le Broc (*broco* means olive-cutting) was quite popular with a number of bishops who sought relaxation here. This splendidly located village possesses an idyllic plaza with arcaded buildings. There is also a fountain whose cool waters have saved more than a few hikers, coming over the mountain from St Jeannet, from heat exhaustion – including me! You can best tame your growling stomach at **Chez Guy**: the pizza, topped with strictly fresh ingredients, is reasonably priced and has a flavour delightfully suggestive of a wild mountain landscape.

Bouyon, once a border village between Nice and Savoy, has only 229 residents. These are mostly senior citizens, since the younger people have left in search of employment. It's probably for this reason that so many houses are for sale around the rectangular village plaza. Speculators will almost certainly be rewarded for their risk in a few years. The view is fantastic over the Cheiron, the Var and Esteron Valleys and the Alps of the French-Italian border region.

Now you should take the D8 through ever more wild and deserted countryside along the Chiers mountain-range, to arrive at **Bezaudun-les-Alpes**, where the fabulous old doors could almost induce enthusiasts to commit criminal deeds by discreetly stealing them away by moonlight. Above the gorge of the River Cagne, the tall façades of the houses of **Coursegoules** seem to reach for the sky. If you are lucky enough to find the church door unlocked, you should spend a couple of minutes admiring the panels painted by the omnipresent local artist Louis Bréa.

Drive back to Vence on the D2, high above the River Cagne, which swells during periods of heavy rain and can then boast some beautiful waterfalls. The road passes the **Ranch El Bronco** (tel: 93 58 09 83) where horse-riders can set out, with a guide, for a lovely ride through a spartan but charming thyme-scented landscape. Af-

terwards, saddle-sore, weary and hungry, you can enjoy a meal at the simple tables of the ranch, where the salad is made with an outstandingly good olive oil. (For those interested in riding elsewhere on the Riviera, the What to Know section of this book features riding on page 116, with stables listed in 11 areas.)

Just past the **Col-de-Vence** (altitude 3,700ft/1,128m), drive as slowly as possible to admire the unique view. From here you can survey the whole mountain chain between the right bank of the Var and Mont Agel, and the coast from Cap Ferrat, past Nice and the Baie des Anges, the Antibes peninsula, the islands off Cannes, and right along to the Esterel.

Local cyclists, of whom there are many, will appreciate your driving slowly along these difficult roads. In their brightly coloured outfits they swoop down the mountain, mostly in groups, towards Vence. When you think of the effort it must have taken to pedal up to the pass, you won't mind making way for their hair-raising downhill race.

ST Paul → Canne

ST Paul

10. Steeped in the Tradition of Art

St Paul, a traditional artists' colony; handicrafts in the Rue Grande, the famous Colombe d'Or restaurant, the Fondation Maeght; antiques in La Colle-sur-Loup; the horse-racing track in Cagnes-sur-Mer. (Nice 12 miles/20 km, Vence 3 miles/5 km; allow half a day).

Gently rolling hills and fertile valleys, which have unfortunately become densely settled, surround the hill on which perches **St Paul-de-Vence**, a village originally built as a border fortification in the 16th century.

In the 1920s St Paul was discovered by painters like Signac, Bonnard, Modigliani and Soutine. These young and as yet unknown artists lodged in the modest *auberge* at the entrance to the village,

64

where they were able to pay with their paintings, a fact which got around quickly. Derain, Utrillo, Vlaminck and Matisse came, followed by young intellectuals such as Prévert, Camus, Giono, Maeterlinck, Morand and Kipling, who transformed the village into a sort of St-Germain-des-Près-de-la-Mer. In the 1940s people from the cinema industry joined the party. Today it is difficult to imagine the peace and quiet of this once so typical Provençal village, especially as it is now one of the most popular tourist destinations in France.

Only residents are allowed to drive into St Paul, and even then they are limited to the road running round the edge. Leave your car well outside, and stroll along the **Rue Grande**, the narrow cobble-stoned main street which cuts through the length of the village. In the almost too perfectly restored old streets and houses, decorated with their coats of arms, you will find endless arts and crafts shops and galleries. You should get up early if you want to enjoy the atmosphere undisturbed by the multilingual chattering of the crowds as they pile out of their coaches later in the day. You will be glad you made the effort as you admire the little square with the urn-shaped fountain and the vaulted washing-house, glimpse inside a church, spend a couple of minutes at Chagall's grave and make your way back along the village wall, past won-derful gardens hidden behind high walls and full of orange trees, to the **Café de la Place**, where you can get an especially good *café crème* and skim the pages of *Nice Matin* (the local newspaper). In front of the café you will undoubtedly see the locals playing *boules*, which is a passion for many of them. Among them you may well see the old man who uses a magnet to pick up the heavy iron balls, as he has difficulty bending over.

St Paul's urn-shaped fountain

Many of those whom I associate closely with St Paul are sadly no longer there: Lino Ventura, James Baldwin, Chagall, Kurt Jürgens, Yves Montand... and La Mère Roux, proprietor of the renowned restaurant the **Colombe d'Or**, the white-haired old lady who radiated so much dignity. Her portrait hangs in the bar of that simple *auberge* that artists used to flock to, and indeed still do. Lunch or

Boules players, St Paul

Inside the Colombe d'Or

dinner on the terrace of the Colombe d'Or is still one of the Côte d'Azur's truly magic experiences. Be sure to reserve a table (tel: 93 32 80 02), and sample the 15 *hors d'oeuvres*, leaving room for the main course, and the Grand Marnier soufflé for dessert. Afterwards stroll through the dining-room with its painted wooden ceiling and walls hung with works by Picasso, Miro, Dufy, Chagall, Matisse, and out to the garden where a huge mosaïc by Léger adorns the wall, alongside a Calder mobile. The hotel itself has a charming, almost cosy atmosphere.

A visit to the **Fondation Maeght** is an absolute must, even for those who are not great art-lovers. Art-dealers Aimé and Marguerite Maeght created this beautiful and lively museum of modern art with the help of architect José Luis Sert. The two main buildings joined by an entrance hall are constructed in a light-coloured concrete and red brick, and adorned with a basin-like roof design which is reminiscent of a Mediterranean rain storage tank. In addition to the museum's own considerable collection there are significant additional exhibitions each year which are based on a particular theme or the work of a contemporary painter. There is also a bookshop, library and cinema.

Around the two buildings the gardens have been landscaped and contain a gigantic sculpture by Calder, a variety of mobiles, a fountain with moving metal cylinders, and other sculptures and ceramics. (Open 10am–7pm; closed 12.30–2.30pm October to June). Just a short walk from St Paul; go down the main road from the village towards La Colle-sur-Loup and take the first turning right).

Leaving St Paul, drive back down to Cagnes-sur-Mer via **La Colle-sur-Loup**, where the main street is a row of antique shops. When you arrive in Cagnes-sur-Mer, you should drive down to the coast and turn right towards Antibes. Immediately on the right is the **Hippodrome de la Côte d'Azur**, the Riviera's famous horse-racing track. If you feel so inclined you can try your luck for as

Fondation Maeght

little as five francs, although of course you don't have to bet to enjoy a visit to the races. Racing takes place mid-December to mid-March in normal daylight hours, and in the cooler evenings during July and August.

Further along the coast you can't help but notice the pyramid-shaped **Marina Baie des Anges** apartment complex, visible from many miles away. Its modern architecture has been the subject of controversy. From their plant-hung terraces, owners of the penthouse-like condominiums can keep an eye on their boats, which are moored in the 'most beautiful yacht harbour in the world' as is modestly proclaimed at the entrance to the residential complex. Whether the Marina is beautiful is open to question, but it is certainly a landmark.

Château Villeneuve

11. Villeneuve-Loubet and Escoffier

To Villeneuve-Loubet, the medieval château and the Musée d'Art Culinaire (open afternoons only); Marineland; the Siesta. (Nice 10 miles/16 km; Cannes 14 miles/23 km; Antibes 8 miles/12 km; Vence 8 miles/12 km).

There is a good view of the Baie des Anges from the old town of Villeneuve-Loubet. Just off the N7 and only a mile (2km) from the coast on the left bank of the Loup, it can seem a long way from the crowds. The medieval streets are tucked around the **Château Villeneuve**, built in the 12th century with a 100-ft (30-metre) tower. The Peace Treaty of Nice was signed here in 1538 and the castle was restored in the 19th century. Today it is privately owned and cannot be visited.

The **Musée d'Art Culinaire** was founded in 1966 with the aim of establishing a museum of culinary arts in the house in which the 'king of chefs and chef of kings' was born, in recognition of the services which Auguste Escoffier rendered to the world of cuisine. As well as a typical Provençal kitchen and a display of Escoffier's own cooking utensils, the museum includes an exhibition of 15,000 menus, some of which date back to 1820, and an interesting display of cookery books, including one of my own.

The most important meeting of Escoffier's life was with César Ritz, for whom he first worked in 1883 in the Grand Hotel in Monte Carlo. When Ritz took over the Savoy in London, this became the meeting-place for high society, thanks largely to Escoffier. In 1898 Ritz opened the establishment which bears his name in Paris. Again, it was to Escoffier that the hotel owed its immediate success. In 1899 he followed Ritz to London's Carlton, which he did not leave until 1920, when he finally returned to Monte Carlo aged 74. He died on February 12, 1935. He is known for having

Musée de l'Art Culinaire

created the peach melba, but it is perhaps less well-known that he developed the stock cube with Julius Maggi, now a basis for cuisine the world over.

On the road from Villeneuve-Loubet to Antibes you will pass **Marineland**, which started out as a sort of aquatic zoo and puts on daily shows with dolphins, sea-lions and killer whales. The complex has grown to include mini-golf, a butterfly jungle, a little farm and an aqua park. Opposite is a huge fairground which is open from late afternoon all summer. Visitors with children will surely not be allowed to sneak past it!

On the beach between Antibes and Marina Baie des Anges you can't miss the **Siesta**, an open-air nightclub with restaurant, casino and seven dance-floors, one of which is in the form of lily leaves in the middle of a pool: definitely for early-on in the evening, although with the price of drinks you may well still be in a fit state to rock and roll your way around, even in the early hours. Admission and your first drink will cost about 130FF, which is standard for nightclubs on the Côte d'Azur.

The old and the new: the historical village of Valbonne and Sophia Antipolis High Technology Park. (Cannes 8 miles/13km; Antibes 10 miles/17km; Mougins 4 miles/7km; Nice 18 miles/30km.)

'Vallis bona' (Happy Valley) has been cultivated since antiquity. The history of the village of **Valbonne** itself dates back to the 13th century when the Chalais order founded the monastery which is now the church on the river-bank below the village. The village centre is the beautiful **Place des Arcades**, shaded by old elm trees. The pretty old fountain is worth a look.

Valbonne owes its modern-day importance to senator Pierre Lafitte, the former director of the highly respected Paris School of Engineering. On a wooded plateau south-east of Valbonne, he founded the international **Sophia Antipolis Science Park** for research and non-polluting industry.

Inspired by the American Silicon Valley example, Lafitte declared, 'One day this region will be considered the California of Europe.' It is conveniently located for access to Nice Côte d'Azur International Airport – the second busiest in France – and the A8 motorway that runs along the coast.

The park has attracted hundreds of national and international companies providing thousands of jobs and there have been optimistic forecasts that hi-tech industries here will overtake tourism by the 21st century. With pleasant residential areas close by, sporting facilities and cultural centres, Sophia Antipolis has plenty to offer its scientists and business workers.

Kitsch to Kitchenware

Antibes

13. Artists and Shipbuilders

The Château Grimaldi and the Musée Picasso; the Cathedral; the covered market on the Cours Masséna; Plage de la Gravette; Port Vauban Yacht harbour; the Restaurant Régal. (Cannes 7 miles/11km; Nice 14 miles/22km; half a day).

'I paint Antibes, a small fortified city. Entirely in the gleam of the sun, it rises up from the beautiful mountains and the eternally snow-covered ranges of the Alps. One ought to paint it with gold and precious gems.' These are the enthusiastic words of Claude Monet, who resided in **Antibes** in 1888. However, in contrast to the paintings Picasso left to the city under the condition that they could never be lent out, the 36 paintings Monet produced here are now in the United States.

The Greek city of Antipolis (Antibes) was founded at the same time as Nikaia (Nice). The city fell into the possession of King Henry IV at the end of the 14th century, when, realising its strategic importance on the border of France and Savoy, he began fortification work which was finally completed in the 17th century by Vauban. Today the ramparts that form the sea-wall and the **Fort Carré** are all that is left. The view from the fortified walls is spectacular, although it is questionable whether Napoleon would have appreciated it when he was held as a prisoner in the Fort Carré after the fall of Robespierre. Painters and writers fleeing Hitler were also interned in the fort.

The **Château Grimaldi** was constructed in the 12th century, in the design of an ancient Roman fort. The rectangular tower, battlements and several window openings are all that remain from that period, however, as the rest of the château was rebuilt in the 16th century. It is open to the public as an art museum, and in the chapel you can see the earliest known illustration of the town of Antibes in the background of a 1539 painting by Antoine Aundi. There are works by Germaine Richier, César, Miró and Pagès on the garden terrace which faces the sea, and Arman's predilection for stringed instruments is admirably documented in the interior courtyard. The main attraction, however, is the **Musée Picasso**, which is housed in the château. Here you get a sense of the *joie de vivre* and serenity Picasso must have felt during his stay here in 1946. This happiness didn't come out of the blue – the war was finally over, there was the splendid studio, provided by the director of the local museum, the sun and light of the South, a new 'young' love (Françoise Gilot, whose book I recommend), renewed fatherhood and good friends such as Prévert and Eluard.

In addition to Picasso's work the museum possesses a collection of contemporary works by Léger, Magnelli, Hartung and Max Ernst as well as the Russian-French painter Nicolas de Staël. The latter lived in Antibes for some time and is said to have plunged to his death from his terrace in 1955.

Those interested in history may like to visit the **Musée**

Still life in Antibes harbour

Archéologique in the **Bastion St André** constructed by Vauban. Here you can see finds from Antibes and the surrounding area, discovered during excavations on land and at sea. Just next to the Musée Picasso is the Romanesque **Cathedral**.

The covered market (daily except Monday) on the **Cours Masséna** is filled with all the delightful colours, tastes and smells of Provence. If you walk down from the covered market towards the port, you will come to another little square where a flea market is held every Thursday and Saturday. The **Musée Peynet**, located on the **Place**

Plage de la Gravette

Nationale, has drawings of Raymond Peynet's cartoon *Lovers* which are known virtually the world over. You can relax at a café or restaurant terrace under the shade of the plane trees and, with a bit of luck, you might hear a melody floating out of a window recorded by Sidney Bechet, the famous composer and clarinet player, who is buried locally. Around the covered market and along the road continuing down towards the port, there are many cafés and bars with an almost exclusively English clientele. As you reach the port, turn right under the arch and right again through a hole in the harbour wall and you will find the **Plage de la Gravette**, a fine sandy beach in a sheltered bay.

Antibes has four yacht harbours with almost 3,000 berths. The most magnificent luxury yachts are moored in the modern **Port Vauban Yacht Harbour**, located near the harbour offices. The boats look like something out of *1001 Nights* – which is also the name of the quay on which they're tied up. George Nicholson, one of the best-known shipbuilders, knows the yachts, their owners, and their histories. He will tell you that Adnan Kashoggi, for example, owner of the *Nabila*, really loved the sea and spent six months a year on his yacht. Countless gossip columnists made a living from reporting his parties.

Donald Trump bought the *Nabila* and renamed it *Princess Trump*. When he found out that it wasn't the largest yacht in the world, he came unhappily to Nicholson: 'Could you lengthen it for me?' he wanted to know in all seriousness. The yacht has since been lengthened.

Nonetheless the *Princess Trump* is still smaller than the royal yacht *Britannia*, of the British royal family, and smaller than Stavros Niarchos's *Atlantis*, which docks in Monte Carlo harbour. One of the largest belongs to King Fahd of Saudi Arabia.

In my opinion the most beautiful yacht around at the moment is the *Corinthia*, berthed at Porto Canto in Cannes. People still talk about the party that the Prince de Lignac gave on his *New Horizon I* at St Tropez' Pampelonne Beach: even if the Prince isn't *really* a prince, his ship certainly resembles a palace. The *Stalca* belongs to the royal family of Monaco and is named after Stéphanie, Albert and Caroline.

The wines of the Ott estate are among the most famous in Provence. Anne Ott manages **Le Mas de la Pagane** (tel: 93 33 33 78), an enchanting little hotel with country charm, surprisingly located within walking distance of Antibes railway station.

14. Cap d'Antibes – El Dorado of Luxury

Cap d'Antibes, the Restaurant du Bacon; the popular holiday town of Juan-les-Pins; Golfe-Juan. (Tour of the peninsula roughly 6 miles/10km – allow 2 hours; with Juan-les-Pins and Golfe-Juan allow half a day.)

The gorgeous **Cap d'Antibes**, whose name was immortalised by F. Scott Fitzgerald, lies between Antibes and Juan-les-Pins. On the Antibes side, the **Salis** beach affords swimmers a splendid view of

The entrance to Jardin Thuret

the old town of Antibes backed by the Alps. A drive, or better still, a walk, around the Cap is well worthwhile. Here and there between the famous luxury hotels and villas you can see large greenhouses, mostly growing carnations, small Provençal country houses and even a children's summer camp.

The **Restaurant du Bacon** is known for its excellent fish dishes. A footpath leads up from the coast to the highest point on the Cap. From here you can see from the Esterel to the Alps, and there is a lighthouse whose beams reach my bedroom in Vence. The **Plage de la Garoupe** is set on a very pretty bay, but it is almost impossible to get to the beach itself for all the private restaurants and their mattresses. Behind the beach is the lovely **Jardin Thuret**, where some of the first eucalyptus trees to be introduced to Europe were brought from Australia and planted here during the middle of the 19th century.

Continuing round the Cap, right out on the southern point is the exclusive **Hôtel du Cap**, whose illustrious guests of the 1920s introduced the summer season to the Riviera. The hotel continues to attract famous guests today, especially during the Cannes Film Festival. Anthony Quinn, Lauren Bacall, Sylvester Stallone and Madonna are just a few of the wel-known stars that have spent the night here.

A little further on you come to the **Musée Naval et Napoléonien** which awakens memories of the French Emperor who landed here after escaping from Elba.

Juan-les-Pins is set in a beautiful sheltered bay. A holiday town particularly popular with young people, it is famous for its long beach of white sand, its attractive yacht and fishing harbour, and its nightlife.

Unfortunately the old casino was demolished, and now the little balls roll in an ultramodern palace of blue glass. The grove with the hundred-year-old pines with which American Florence Gould fell in love (see *History and Culture*, page 16), creates the setting for the annual open-air **Jazz Festival** featuring many great international names.

The two street-cafés **Pam-Pam** and **Le Festival** are open into the early morning hours. Night-owls can quench their thirst with exotic cocktails while steamy Latin American rhythms thunder out of oversized loudspeakers at 150 decibels. With the long business hours here, those who feel that they simply *must* down another cocktail before moving on to a disco or casino won't have any problem. The delightful garden of the **Auberge de l'Esterel** (21 Rue Iles, Tel: 93 61 86 55) is a good alternative for anyone who likes things a bit quieter.

Golfe-Juan has a new harbour for yachts and fishing-boats, a sandy beach which was still almost deserted in Picasso's days, as well as a beautiful view over to the Lérins islands and the Cap d'Antibes. On the beach over on the west side of town is **Tetou** (tel: 93 63 71 16), the chic, and not cheap, place to go for *bouillabaisse*. Reservations are essential and credit cards are not accepted.

Tetou at Golfe-Juan

15. Vallauris – Ceramics, Art and Kitsch

Vallauris, the 'Ceramic Capital'; Picasso's 'War and Peace' in the Romanesque chapel. (Cannes 4 miles/6km; Antibes 5 miles/8km; Nice 20 miles/31km. Allow 2–3 hours.)

Vallauris, just over a mile (2km) northwest of Golfe-Juan, was already a thriving potter's town in Roman times, on account of the red clay it is built upon. In the 16th century the tradition was continued by Italian potters brought in by the bishop from Grasse. But without the influence of Picasso, Vallauris would certainly not have developed to become known to visitors as the 'Ceramic Capital', as it is today.

Picasso moved to Vallauris in 1947 with the love of his life Françoise Gilot, and they lived in the Villa La Galloise until 1955. It was here that Picasso first turned his hand to pottery, and for the first two years he worked at the Madoura pottery work-shop, whose owners, Suzanne and Georges Ramié he had met on the beach in Golfe-Juan. His output was tremen-dous, producing over 2,000 pieces during his first year alone.

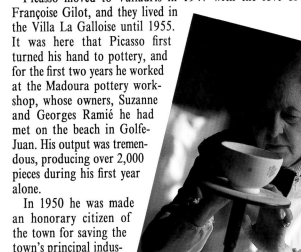

In 1950 he was made an honorary citizen of the town for saving the town's principal indus-try. He repaid the honour by presenting the town with a life-size bronze statue of a man holding a sheep, which now stands outside the church in the **Place Paul Isnard**. The artist regarded it as an important work. 'I did this statue in an single afternoon, but not until after months of reflection and I don't know how many sketches...it was much too weak; it wouldn't hold...I had intended to work on it again, but I didn't have the time.'

The **Musée de Vallauris** is in the château, originally a 13th-century priory that was rebuilt in the 16th century. All that remains of the original priory is the Romanesque chapel, which, in 1952, Picasso decorated with his work *War and Peace*. The museum houses lithographs by Picasso, and ceramics designed by the artist and produced by the Galerie Madoura, as well as a number of works by Alberto Magnelli (who lived and worked in Florence between 1888 and 1971).

In the same year that I made my first visit to France, with my father, I also made my first visit to Picasso. I fell eternally love with both Pablo, the man and artist, and with Vallauris, a romantic little town set on gently rolling hills. My love for Picasso has remained, but not for Vallauris. Françoise Gilot, his former lifetime companion, has very clearly expressed a feeling which I share: 'Pablo's presence brought the town affluence, but his example was not understood. Today Vallauris is a stronghold of bad taste.'

Countless ceramic workshops and stores sell huge amounts of kitsch, with pottery shops lining the whole of Rue Clemenceau. Today over 200 potters live in Vallauris, and since 1966 an international biennial for ceramic art has been held here. The **Galerie Madoura**, owned by the Ramiés' son, is still among the best pottery workshops in town. Besides their own creations they also produce copies of Picasso's works, which are easily confused for originals by unsuspecting tourists.

Picasso left Vallauris in 1955. On the occasion of his 90th birthday the town put on a huge folk-festival, in which the artist, however, declined to take part. He explained: 'I am helpful for your spectacle, but I don't want to *be* your spectacle.' He watched the festival on television.

If you want to spend longer in Vallauris and need refreshment, you can get good food in the **Gousse d'Ail**, 11 Avenue Grasse; tel: 93 64 10 71.

16. Glamour and Money

Belle Epoque buildings, high society, festivals and culinary delights, the Croisette – the internationally-famous shoreline promenade, the Palais des Festivals, the old harbour, seafood at Astoux et Brun, shopping on the Rue d'Antibes. Allow a day.

Cannes' reputation for glamour and sophistication is known the world over. In this respect, little has changed in well over a hundred years. It all started in 1834, when Lord Brougham discovered the little fishing village by chance. Due to a cholera epidemic, he and his daughter were forced, against their will, to stay in an *auberge* in the lower Suquet (old town). He was so pleased by the *bouillabaisse* served there, the harbour, the islands, and the pines and olive groves, that he never arrived in Nice, his original destination, and instead settled in Cannes. For the next 34 years the ex-Chancellor of England spent the winter in the Villa Eléonore. He started a trend among European aristocracy, which soon turned the Roman harbour of Portus Canuae into an international seaside resort. By 1870 the city already had 35 hotels and 200 villas.

'Princes, princes, nothing but princes' groaned de Maupassant, who frequently sailed in the bay of La Napoule between 1884 and 1888. 'If you like them, you're in the right place.' In Cannes, the architects of the Belle Epoque had the opportunity to realise their

wildest dreams. Sumptuous villas, extravagant palaces and fantastic gardens appeared on the hills of La Californie, La Croix-des-Gardes, Le Cannet and Super-Cannes. The **Villa Alexandra**, with its minarets, could be mistaken for a mosque; **Château Scott** is Gothic in style; the **Villa Camille Amélie** has a natural grotto and huge marble columns; the **Villa Yakimour** was built by the Aga Khan for Yvette Labrousse.

Today Cannes' fame stems largely from its role as a media city, with the Film Festival joined by the TV Festival (MIPTV) and the Record and Music Festival (MIDEM). Around 50,000 visitors come every year for the Film Festival alone. The town's motto is '*La Vie est un Festival*', and there is indeed plenty going on here all year round.

Gourmets have come here to be spoiled by some of the world's greatest chefs: Sylvain Duparc in the **Carlton**, Christian Willer in the **Martinez** and Jacques Chibois in the **Royal Gray**, but those looking for something a little less up-market will also find a restaurant to their taste among the over 300 restaurants on the Avenue Félix-Faure, around Forville Market, in the Suquet quarter, on the Quai St Pierre and in the streets between the Croisette and the Rue d'Antibes. Everywhere you go there is a wonderful aroma of garlic, truffles, herbs and spices. The local cuisine is, in the words of poet

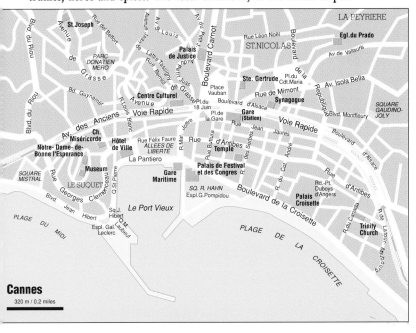

Cannes

320 m / 0.2 miles

Stéphen Liégeard, '*comme une tranche de soleil sur une nappe de mer bleue*' (like a spot of sunlight on a cloth of blue sea).

The **Croisette** must be one of the most internationally-known shoreline promenades in the world. Its cosmopolitan nature is attested by the 96 newspapers in 30 different languages that are on sale. This magnificent boulevard, with its majestic palms and elegant

The most beautiful hotel in Cannes

colourful gardens and parks, stretches from **Palm Beach** (now closed) to the **Palais des Festivals**. Take a stroll along the Croisette, with the sandy beaches on one side decked out in summer with cheerful beach mats and parasols and their restaurants open for lunch. On the other side are luxury boutiques and terrace cafés. Sit for a while on a bench or chair and admire the palatial hotels, the *monstres sacrés* (holy monsters) of the Belle Epoque: the Carlton, the Majestic and the Martinez, all of which have been completely renovated. The most beautiful is still the Carlton, with its white wedding-cake façade and twin domes which, as the story goes, were inspired by the perfect breasts of La Belle Otéro, a courtesan of the coast at the turn of the century.

The Palais des Festivals, which is where the main events of the Film Festival take place, also houses a casino, a nightclub and restaurant, and a gigantic underground car park with 950 parking places. Locally known as the 'bunker', the Palais is a modern complex of glass and concrete whose architecture has stimulated some heated debate. In the old harbour beyond it, fishing boats dock alongside luxury yachts.

Opposite the Palais des Festivals are the **Allées de la Liberté**, an attractive place for a stroll, with a flower market in the mornings and a flea market on Saturdays. Fresh seafood lovers will be spoilt for choice on the Avenue Félix-Faure, but I recommend **Astoux et Brun,** right on the corner at No 27. (tel: 93 39 21 87).

The city's former main traffic artery, the **Rue Meynadier**, connects the city centre with the **Suquet** quarter, the oldest part of town. It is a lively pedestrian shopping street selling clothes and food, including a cheese shop, a pasta shop, two butchers and a *traiteur* who have been awarded medals for the quality of their wares. Forville market (daily except Sundays) is a real feast for the eyes. Not only can you purchase the best fruit, the crispest vegetables and the

The Lérins Islands, home of a well-known 'Son et Lumière'

freshest fish (while rubbing shoulders with Cannes' master-chefs), but you are also taking part in a spectacle which is an integral part of local life.

At the Suquet end of the Rue Meynadier, the **Rue St Antoine**, lined on either side with restaurants, winds its way up to the **Place de la Castre**, where you will find the **Musée de la Castre**, containing archaeological collections and art from the Mediterranean, South America and the Pacific. The square tower (72ft/22metres) once served as a look-out post. If you walk through the old bell tower you come to a shady plaza from which you can look out over the whole of Cannes, the harbour and the islands. Old Cannes around the Suquet consists of only seven or eight little narrow streets.

Head back towards the centre of town, this time on the street running parallel to the Croisette, the **Rue d'Antibes**, Cannes' main shopping street. It is frequently compared to the Rue du Faubourg St-Honoré in Paris, and prices are certainly similar. What was it Cocteau said? 'One can certainly leave the house without an umbrella, but never without one's wallet – the selection is simply too alluring.'

The Beaches

The Croisette: 27 beaches in all, of which seven are public.
Boulevard du Midi: Nearly 3 miles (4.5km) of public beach.
Boulevard Gazagnaire: Large public beach.

Special Events

January: MIDEM (international record and music market).
February: Mimosa festival; International Games Festival.
March: MIPIM (Real Estate); Old-timer exhibition.
April: MIPTV (International TV Programming Market).
May: International Film Festival.
June: Publicity Film Festival; Festival of Cabaret.
July/August: Music evenings in the Le Suquet quarter; *Son et Lumière* on the Lérins Islands; Bridge Festival; Regatta; International Commercial Film Festival.
September: International Boat Week.
October: Tax-Free World; MIPCOM (Communications Festival).
November: The International Dance Festival.

AROUND Cannes

17. Grasse – the city of 'Noses'

In the footsteps of Napoleon; Mougins and its distinguished restaurants; the health-resort town of Grasse, the perfume metropolis, its Cathedral and the old quarter; Musée Fragonard; back to Cannes via Cabris, Spéracèdes and Tanneron. (Approximately 25 miles/40km. Allow a whole day).

After his return from exile in Elba, Napoleon arrived in Cannes, having landed at Golfe-Juan, with a few of his trusted men. The next morning he began his arduous march through the Alps to Grenoble. We follow their course as far as Grasse.

Mougins, amidst a delightful landscape reminiscent of Tuscany, is certainly worth a visit, not only for the many excellent restaurants, the best of which is the **Moulin de Mougins**, featuring the *cuisine du soleil* of master chef Roger Vergé (tel: 93 75 78 24; expensive, book first) and located in an old oil mill, but also because this well-preserved town is among the most beautiful in the region.

Jacques Brel used to live at **71 Rue des Lombards**; the Belgian kings Leopold and Baudoin stayed in the former **Hôtel La Pax**; Yves St Laurent spent his holidays in the **Villa Santa Lucia**, and the Moreaus and Deneuves lived in **La Grâce Dieu**. Picasso spent the last years of his life down the hill near the **Chapelle Notre Dame de la Vie**, which is surrounded by cypresses and olive trees.

'Scent organ', Grasse

Once you've driven past Mouans-Sartoux
you can already begin to make out **Grasse**.
The village was originally a health resort
for the likes of Queen Victoria and Napoleon's sister, Pauline. After Catherine
de Medici imported from Italy the trend
of wearing perfumed gloves, it was a
logical step to begin producing the
necessary scents in Grasse. In the 18th
century there were already several
firms which processed mimosa, nee-
dle furze, and orange flowers, roses,
lavender, jasmine and hyacinths by
the ton into minute amounts of
concentrated essences for the wealthy. Today
Grasse has developed into one of the most important
perfume-manufacturing cities in the world.

You can tour the large perfume factories of **Fragonard** (in the
centre of town), **Galimard** and **Molinard**. The **Musée International
de la Parfumerie** on the Place du Cours covers every aspect of the
industry. It is possible to study the craft of perfume-making at
Foure Bertrand Dupont, a private institute which has trained some
of the best 'noses'.

A tour of the old city will take you about three hours, beginning
behind the **Notre-Dame-du-Puy Cathedral**, where you can see a
triptych by Bréa, a Fragonard and three oil paintings by Rubens.
The old city is still primarily orientated towards the needs of the
locals, which is what makes it particularly interesting for tourists.
The **Place aux Aires** is especially attractive; every morning a vegetable
and flower market is held there.

Jean Honoré Fragonard (1732–1806) was a native of Grasse

whose family intended him to become a notary. But Fragonard had other ideas. Awarded the Prix de Rome at the age of 20, he rapidly progressed to become a fashionable painter of the Paris aristocracy, designing a tapestry for Louis XV. However, he got into financial difficulties when the Revolution took its toll on his clientele and had to return to Grasse. Later he eked out a paltry living in Paris until his death. You can see a few examples of his work as well as a number of pieces by his son and grandson in the **Fragonard Villa-Museum**, the glovemaker's house where he sought refuge during the Revolution.

Take a slightly roundabout but very attractive route back to Cannes, leaving Grasse by the D4 to **Cabris**, where many artists have settled. On Christmas Eve people come from all around to take part in the nativity procession through the village. At **18 Rue**

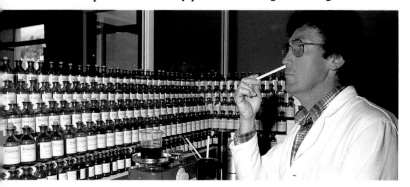

A decisive 'nose'

de la Terrasse you will find authentic and locally-made nativity figures and *santons*, models of saints made out of unfired clay. You might also find yourself drawn to one of the very simple, and thus especially impressive, carved wooden Madonnas which are made by the son of the house. This would make an unusual gift or a lovely souvenir of your stay on the Riviera.

Next take the D11 to **Spéracèdes**, with its mill and wash-houses, and continue on to the D562, where you should turn right towards Draguignan. Branch left on to the D94 which leads you down to the **Auberge de St-Cassien-des-Bois**. Next to the auberge, where coachloads of visitors stop off to eat during the high tourist season, there is a charming chapel dating from the 12th century. If, despite the stern signs forbidding it, you dare to set foot along the path, you will be rewarded by a lovely of a picturesque river valley, a tributary of Lake St Cassien and a rectangular defence tower with only one window. Perhaps this walk is worth the risk of innocent trespassing.

At the next intersection turn left on to the D38, which you should follow through the little-developed Massif de Tanneron with lovely forests of mimosa and eucalyptus. These were replanted after the huge forest fire of 1970. At Mandelieu you join the heavily-travelled N7 which leads back to Cannes.

Marionnette shop in
Tourrettes sur Loup

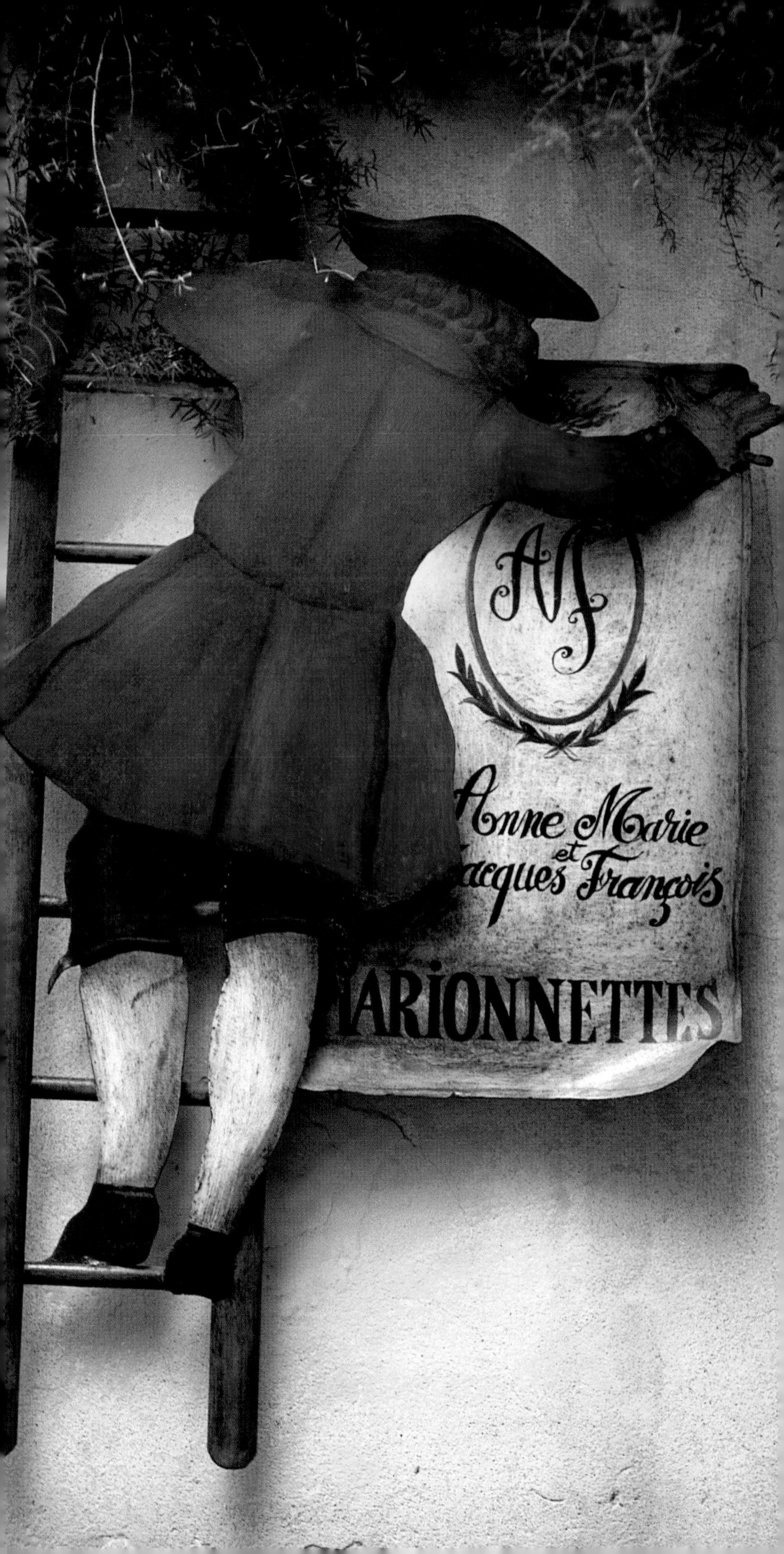
AJF
Anne Marie
et
Jacques François
MARIONNETTES

Cannes → ST TROPEZ

18. Coast of Red Cliffs

The Esterel mountains; Théoule with its yacht harbour and beaches;
the exclusive seaside resort of Miramar; views from the coastal
road; St Raphael and the neighbouring historic town of Fréjus.
(About 28 miles/45km. Allow a whole day – especially in summer
and at weekends when the road is busy.)

Massif de l'Esterel

The **Corniche d'Or**, which passes through a landscape of unique
beauty, was laid out in 1903 on the initiative of the Touring-Club
de France. This section of the coast is completely different from
the stretch between Menton and Cannes. Here the imposing Esterel
mountains, around 1,000ft (300m) high, with their wild red cliffs
of volcanic stone, have prevented development. The landscape is
dominated by spruces, pines, chestnuts, eucalyptus trees and cork-
oaks; numerous little coves tempt you to take a swim, and footpaths
lead up to the summits from where you can survey the whole of
this dramatic coastline.

The highest peak is **Mont Vinaigre** (2,027ft/618m). In the olden
days mailcoaches were regularly held up and robbed at this point.
The mountain range is cut by deep gorges which extend down to
the sea, where the waves break against vertical rock walls, indented
capes, minute inlets and *calanques* (fjord-like bays). They also wash
up against semi-submerged rocks and green islands.

As you follow the coast road out of Cannes, you come first to

La Sagne Montblanc Les Mujouls Sigale Roquesteron Pierrefeu Bonson
Brianconnet Gars Aiglun *Estéron* Conségudes Les Ferres Gilette
St.Auban MONTAGNE DE CHARAMEL Le Mas *Girande* *Estéron* Gréolières-les-Neiges DU CHEIRON Bouyon
Le Brunet Les Sausses MONTAGNE Cime du Cheiron 1777 Bézaudun-les-Alpes Mouton d'Anou 1085 Le Broc
La Foux Thorenc Gréolières Coursegoules Carros
Valderoure *Loup* Cipières St. Barnabé St. Jeannet Gattières
Caille Andon MONTAGNE DE L'AUDIBERGUE St. Maurice L'Ecre Col de Vence 970 Vence La Gaude La Barenne
Séranon Caussols Courmes Tourrette-sur-Loup
Esclapon Escragnolles Nans Gourdon St. Paul
Mons St.Vallier-de-Thiey Le Bar *Loup* Le Colle-sur-Loup
Pas de la Faye Magagnosc Le Rouret Roquefort-les-Pins Cagnes
Grottes de St.Cézaire Grasse Châteauneuf-de-Grasse Les Maillans
St-Cézaire-sur-Siagne Cabris Plascassier Valbonne Biot
Fayence Le Tignet Peymeinade Sophia-Antipolis Villeneuve-Loubet-Plage
Tourrettes Montauroux Roquette-sur-Siagne Mouans-Sartoux **Marineland**
Le Bégude Tanneron St.Jean Mougins Vallauris
St.Paul-en-Forêt *Lac de St.Cassien* Pegomas Le Cannet Antibes
Esterel MASSIF DU TANNERON Mandelieu Golfe-Juan
Reyran **Cannes** *Golfe Juan* Cap d'Antibes
Bagnols-en-Forêt Les Adrets de l'Esterel L'Eglise *Golfe de La Napoule* *Ile Ste-Marguerite*
St. Jean Maure-Vieil Théole-sur-Mer
Le Captou **Mont Vinaigre 618** DE L'ESTEREL La Galère *Ile St.Honorat*
Miramar *ILES DE LÉRINS*
Puget-sur-Argens MASSIF Agay L'ESTEREL COTE D'AZUR
Les Tourres Fréjus Valescure Anthéor Plage
Anthéor DE
St.Raphaël Boulouris Le Dramont
Golfe de Fréjus Cap du Dramont
St.Aygulf CORNICHE *Mediterranean*
La Gaillarde
San-Peire-sur-Mer Les Issambres *Sea*
La Nartelle Val d'Esquières COTE D'AZUR

**Corniche
de L'Esterel**

8 miles / 12 km

The holiday settlement of Port La Galère

La Napoule, situated on the banks of the River Siagne at the foot of Mont San Peyré, and part of Mandelieu, which is so famous for its mimosa. The old castle in La Napoule was restored by the American sculptor Henry Clews. The building, which has displays of his work, is open to the public.

The next stop is **Théoule-sur-Mer**, once a busy harbour, and now popular for its sheltered beaches. It is here that Louis Féraud found the inspiration for his wondrously colourful fashion collections, and he commented, 'Here is the cradle of my success, the origin of my creativity.' Eighty percent of the land belonging to the town has been declared a 'green zone', and 65 miles (102km) of hiking paths criss-cross the forested hinterland. Among those who enjoy the peace and quiet here are fashion designer Pierre Cardin, and a couple of Emirs (one of whom owns the Hotel Saint Christophe). Richelieu was also attracted to the area – he had a castle built right on the sea when the Spaniards were in possession of the Lérins Islands. In August the *Nuits de L'Esterel* (concerts and events including folklore presentations and fireworks) are held here.

Above Théoule is a villa which appears to consist of bull's-eye windows stacked on top of each other. It was designed by the Hungarian-born Antti Lovag, a student of the architect Couelle, for his personal use. The house has neither a roof nor a façade in the traditional sense. You can easily climb upon the 'red bullets' and hop from one to the other.

The holiday settlement, **Port La Galère**, is located in a wooded area on a cliff above the bay of La Napoule. The complex was created by Couelle himself, the inventor of 'habitable sculpture'. The peculiar cave-like holes in their exterior walls allow the houses to blend into the cliffs. The beach below is one of the most beautiful on the coast, although it is reserved for residents and guests of the private complex.

The exclusive seaside resort of **Miramar** has a private yacht harbour in La Figueirette Bay. In the 17th century these waters were full of tuna fish, so it is appropriate that the region's first fish farm was established in the bay in 1986; it produces 30 tons of silver bream and bass per year.

As you continue your drive round the coast towards **Anthéor**, there are two places where it is worth stopping your car to admire the view: the **Pointe de l'Observatoire** and the **Pic du Cap Roux**, both of which afford splendid panoramas over the red rocks and deep blue Mediterranean.

The well-protected bay of **Agay**, which is overlooked by the 945-ft (288-m) **Rastel d'Agay**, was a favourite spot of the Ligurians, Greeks and Romans. From here, you can take the deserted roads inland to the **Pic de l'Ours, Mont Vinaigre** and the **Malpey Ranger Station**, where the elegant criminal boss, Gaspard de Besse, managed his shady business in the 18th century. Also hidden in the Esterel Mountains is a lake, which is pleasant for a swim, and an area teeming with wild boar, which won't bother you at all because they are usually too busy eating the bread people bring along to feed them.

Alternatively you can continue along the road to **Valescure**, passing on the way **Cap Esterel**. This is one of the region's gigantic new projects for a holiday centre modelled on a Provençal village, with three-storey houses and no cars.

St Raphael, a pretty little sea-side resort, was originally a Roman holiday centre, before being plundered by the Saracen pirates. In the 10th century it belonged to the Lérins monks, and passed to the custody of the Knights Templar 200 years later. Napoleon landed here on his return from Egypt; he also departed from here 14 years later when he was banished to Elba.

Alphonse Karr, chief editor of *Le Figaro* during the 19th century,

A glass-bottomed boat on the coast

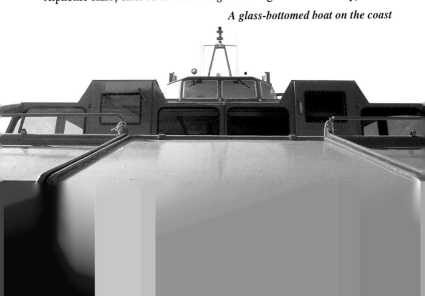

was responsible for St Raphael becoming the fashionable resort it is today. He lived in Nice until he discovered St Raphael, and then he encouraged his friends to follow him down the coast. Those that did include Dumas, de Maupassant, Berlioz and Gounod. The latter composed his *Romeo and Juliet* here. Erika Mann described St Raphael as a 'stately old-fashioned Riviera town', which, with its palm-lined promenade, numerous hotels and casino, was very popular, especially among the British.

Today the city, which has a population of around 30,000, boasts the Santa Lucia convention centre, 'the most beautiful train station in Europe' (only six hours from Paris on the TGV), seven harbours and the **Musée Archéologique** which has a large collection of amphorae. In the garden of the museum stands a Roman milestone from the Via Aurelia.

The neighbouring city of **Fréjus** – Caesar's Forum Julii – was located on an extension of the Via Aurelia which went through Gaul to Spain. Emperor Augustus had galleys built here; he owed his victory over the fleet of Anthony and Cleopatra to the manoeuvrability of these ships.

Around the time of the birth of Christ, Fréjus was the second-largest Roman harbour in the western Mediterranean after Ostia, Rome's outlet to the sea. The Roman **Arena**, originally built to accommodate 10,000 spectators, was one of the oldest in Gaul. Although fairly badly damaged, it is still used today in summer for bullfights and rock concerts. Fréjus (40,000 inhabitants) is larger than St Raphael has far more souvenirs of its long past.

The ancient **episcopal city** (the guided tour is worth taking and lasts about 45 minutes) is in the centre of present-day Fréjus at the Place Formigé. It includes a 4th-century baptistry, the Cathedral which dates partly from the 10th century and partly from the 12th, a 13th-century cloister and the former bishop's palace which now houses the town hall. Today, despite the modern beach-front stretch and the new harbour, Fréjus has more the feel of an inland town than a port. However, **Fréjus Plage** is a development of apartment blocks and hotels running the length of a fine flat sandy beach by the new yacht basin of Port Fréjus. By night the cafés, shops and stalls here are particularly popular. The harbour at **Port Fréjus** has mooring for 700 yachts. An ambitious projected stage of the development is to open up a channel, originally dug by the Romans which will lead into the centre of the town, connecting it to the sea as in Roman times.

The Argens Valley separates the Massif de l'Esterel from the Massif des Maures, where your next itinerary will take you.

Massif des Maures

19. From Fréjus to St Tropez

A picnic in the beautiful Massif des Maures; the holiday resort of St Aygulf, fashionable Ste Maxime; Port Grimaud – the 'Venice of Provence'. (22 miles/35km. Allow all day, with the morning in the Maures, and the afternoon to get to St Tropez.)

Contrary to popular belief, the **Massif des Maures** was not named after the Moorish invaders, but is rather a derivation of the Greek *amauros*, which was corrupted in the Provençal dialect to *maouro* meaning gloomy or dark. This explanation seems more poetic to me, since dark forests are an essential characteristic of the Massif: oak forests with an underbrush consisting of gorse and myrrh bushes, briars (the roots of which are made into smoking pipes), pine forests, chestnut groves and the cork-oaks whose bark is cut off every seven years to produce stoppers for bottles.

It is beautiful and lonely in these forests, whose gently rolling hills are interspersed here and there with olive trees, sheep grazing amid crimson poppies and the occasional field filled with rows of vines. Olives, bread, sheep's cheese and a bottle of good red wine – such a picnic befits the landscape and forms an exquisite pleasure in its simplicity. The contrast between the bustling resort towns and this quiet landscape couldn't be greater. Only a short distance away from the hubbub you feel as though you're in another world.

When you have had your fill, return to the coast at St Aygulf for the drive to St Tropez, which you should aim to reach shortly after sunset.

St Aygulf is a little resort town with a beautiful, long sandy beach – one of the Riviera's few remaining relatively unspoilt stretches of sand. West of the town, you can climb down the cliffs to the little hidden beaches of **Les Issambres, San Peïre, Val d'Esquières** and **La Garonnette**. These are all perfect places for a late-afternoon swim.

The **Gulf of St Tropez** begins at **St Maxime** – where the villas become large again, and you re-enter the land of the obviously rich and famous. This fashionable resort town is picturesquely situated on the north shore of the bay. It has fishing and yachting harbours, as well as a sandy beach. The restored **old quarter** is reserved for pedestrians in the afternoons during the high season. The Lérins monks erected the rectangular tower in front of the harbour for defence purposes. Later it served as a court building and today it houses the **Musée des Traditions Locales**. The **church** has an interesting altar made of green marble from the Charterhouse of La Verne (see *page 95*). The choir pew dates from the 15th century.

Six miles (10km) inland on the D25 towards Le Muy, the **Museum of Phonographs and Mechanical Musical Instruments** has an interesting collection of over 300 musical automatons.

Guy de Maupassant's family once lived in the Villa Béthanie, not far from the casino, to the left past the Traverse Granier. Ste Maxime is an active little town, with five nightclubs, a casino and many different festivals and events (folklore, concerts, fireworks and exhibitions), not to mention the usual Riviera choice of restaurants. I recommend the **Hermitage** (tel: 94 96 17 77) on the harbour, where they serve a delicious sea-bass with fennel.

Port Grimaud is situated at the far end of the bay. It was designed during the 1950s and 60s by architect François Spoerry, who obtained

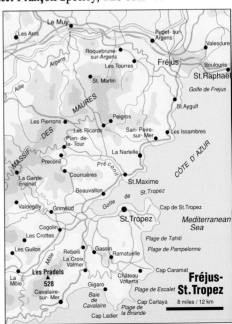

a piece of marshland at the mouth of the River Giscle in 1962 and then had to wait four years to get planning permission. The inspiration is typically Provençal, but each house has a waterfront and a boat mooring. In theory cars are not allowed inside the village, and transport is provided by boats. Some 2,500 colourfully painted houses line the streets, shady, flower-filled squares invite you to linger a while and small bridges span the canals. At the beginning of the 1990s Port Grimaud was France's third most popular tourist attraction. Although Gri-

Port Grimaud

maud is sometimes regarded as childishly contrived, it is a successful example of contemporary architecture. So successful that a second village, **Port Cogolin**, is being constructed just along the coast. It is a far cry from the concrete and glass horrors bordering the Mediterranean elsewhere.

Just 3 miles (5km) inland, the beautifully kept medieval village of **Grimaud** is located below the ruins of its fortress. The serpentine portals and basalt arcades in the Rue du Templier are impressive.

20. Outing to La Garde-Freinet

A picturesque Provençal village in an idyllic landscape, a hikers' paradise; dining on the terrace of La Faucado. (About 12 miles/20km to La Garde Freinet. Allow half a day, or more if you continue to the Charterhouse de la Verne.)

La Garde Freinet, formerly named Fraxinet, is situated in the heart of the Massif des Maures in a natural forest area. The village, located at an altitude of about 1,300ft (400m) between the fertile Argens Plain and the Gulf of St Tropez, was occupied by the Saracens for over a century. They taught the people of Provence how to use cork-oak and produce pine tar, and they introduced ceramic tiles and the tambourine to the area. They built a fortress on the hill above the village which served as the starting point for their plundering raids – until the courageous Count William of Arles finally managed to drive the Saracens out permanently in 973AD.

The village is worthy of exploration with its many fountains and

94

little alleyways as well as its Renaissance church and old wash-house. At the entrance to the village is the **Maison de la Garde-Freinet** – the former Chapelle St Eloi – where, alongside handicrafts, you can also buy cheese, honey, wine, preserves and candied sweet chestnuts. The area is a hikers' paradise. The walk up to the fortress ruins takes about half an hour, for which you are rewarded with a splendid view. It takes 20 minutes to get to the **Roches Blanches** – the White Rocks. Further hiking excursions can be made to the charming hamlets of La Mourre, Valdegilly, Nid du Duc, Bas-Olivier, Camp de la Suyère, Val d'Aubert and Gagnal. A brochure with hiking routes is available at the tourist office. A delightful place for a meal is the terrace of **La Faucado** (tel: 94 43 60 41). Here, amidst the wonderful countryside, the fillet of beef in port and served with morel mushrooms tastes especially good.

The famous **Charterhouse of La Verne**, founded in 1170 and abandoned by the monks in 1792, is only about 20 miles (30km) away. Heading back towards Grimaud, turn right onto the D48 and after a mile or so (2km), right again on to the D14. It is a beautiful road, running through chestnut groves and cork-oak forests. The rough road to the Charterhouse turns off to the left.

The following festivals in La Garde Freinet have retained much of their original character:

1 May	St Clément Bravade (parade).
Mid-June	Maure Forest festival.
15 August	Village festival in La Moure with parade.
Late October	Chestnut festival.

The coastline by St Tropez

ST TROPEZ

21. Den of Iniquity – or Fishing Village?

View from the Citadel; a game of boules on the Place des Lices; a drink on a waterfront terrace; typical country fare at Lou Révélen, Fuchs or Palmyre. (Anytime – St Tropez is a round-the-clock place.)

If you believe the legend, this port city – located on the southern shore of one of the most beautiful bays on the Côte d'Azur – owes its name to a Roman soldier by the name of Tropez, who was converted to Christianity during the reign of Nero. This cost him his head. His decapitated corpse was placed in a boat with a dog and a rooster (which were supposed to devour it) and abandoned to the waves. However, miraculously, it landed undamaged on the beach of present-day St Tropez.

In memory of the martyr, the *Bravade* takes place every year on 16 May – a spectacular and very loud procession in which a gilded wooden bust of the saint is carried through the city, inspiring the faithful and entertaining others. A second *Bravade*, on 15 June, commemorates the year 1637 when the people of St Tropez fended off an attack by 22 Spanish galleons which were attempting to plunder the town and capture the four royal ships anchored in the harbour. At the end of the 19th century, Guy de Maupassant wrote of this sleepy fishing village: 'What an enchanting and simple daughter of the sea! You can smell the fish-catch, the burning tar, the brine. The scales of sardines glitter on the cobblestones like pearls.' Quite a lot has changed since then, but the enchantment remains to this day.

Paul Signac, who came here to paint, was so enchanted with the town that he decided to stay. He bought the estate called La Hune and invited many painters to come and visit: Matisse, Marquet, Bonnard, Picabia, Van Dongen, Utrillo and Dufy, to name but a few. Their works are exhibited in the **Musée de l'Annonciade** (Place Grammont). In 1925, the author Colette settled on the peninsula. A forerunner of trends to come, she was at the time considered somewhat indelicate: as early as 1907 she appeared topless in a Paris theatre and she used to swim nude in the sea in front of her villa, La Treille Muscate.

Not long after, the first nightclubs for rich tourists were established. The village then grew fashionable. Swashbuckler Errol Flynn and author and diarist Anaïs Nin – one of Henry Miller's muses – were regular guests. After World War II, Jean Cocteau and the Paris literary scene discovered St Tropez, as did the unforgettable Juliette Greco, followed some time later by countless actors, directors and other show-business people. The town's fortune was really sealed in 1959, when Roger Vadim shot *And God Created Woman* starring Brigitte Bardot. BB bought La Madrague estate, only 1,000ft (300m) from Colette's former residence. Although the author sold her house in 1938, Bardot lives here to this day with her many pets, despite the tourist invasion. In the month of August alone more than 80,000 visit St Tropez, a town which has only 6,250 residents during the winter.

Brigitte Bardot isn't the only person who has stayed in St Tropez: the film director Roger Vadim – who was already familiar with the village before he met Bardot – spends

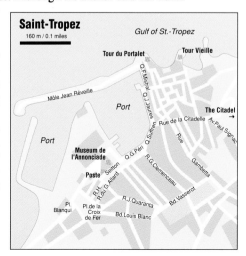

Saint-Tropez
160 m / 0.1 miles

Gulf of St.-Tropez

Tour du Portalet
Tour Vieille
Môle Jean Réveille
Port
Q.F.Mistral
Q.J.Jaurès
Rue de la Citadelle
The Citadel
Av.Paul Signac
Port
Museum de l'Annonciade
Q.G.Péri
Rue
Poste
B.H. Seitton
R.du G.Allard
Q.G.Pétri
R.G.Clemenceau
Gambetta
Pl. Blanqui
Pl.de la Croix de Fer
R.J.Quaranta
Bd.Louis Blanc
Bd.Vasserot

Only on the Côte d'Azur...

three months here every year and stays with one of his numerous ex-wives; Jean-Pierre Aumont, Hollywood's 'French Lover' and writer, acquired a taste for the village when he visited Colette; he still lives above the bay in his Villa San Genesto today.

It is easy to understand the attraction. St Tropez has a unique charm that it manages to retain even in the summer months when it is overrun with tourists. It is the only town on the Riviera facing northwards, which gives a special quality to the evening sunlight as it reflects off the dull-pink and ochre walls. This is one reason why so many painters came here and were inspired by their surroundings, and why so many visitors were inspired to paint for the first time.

If you climb up the hill to the **citadel** at sunset and take in the view of the bay, the harbour and the town with its narrow alleyways and the grey-green tower of the church, then you will recognise the 'colourful shadows' which so fascinated Bonnard. Wander through the old streets and you will see that behind the scenes life goes on

The Citadel

much as it always has in this once sleepy little fishing village: at the authentic fish-market near the quay, in the cafés with their worn-out table-tops, in the arcaded **Rue de la Miséricorde**, the **Rue Allard** and on the **Place des Lices**.

Fish used to be cleaned in the shade of the plane trees on the Place des Lices; now a market is held there on Tuesdays and Saturday mornings and the locals play *boules* with the *coco parisien du showbiz*, as they affectionately refer to Parisian show-business people. To keep posted on the gossip, locals hang out in the **Café des Arts**; as tourists you would do better to listen to Radio St-Tropez (89.5FM). St Tropez still has around a dozen fishing boats which make daily deliveries to the restaurants and the little fish market – thus preserving its status as a fishing village. The work of the fishermen is not made any easier by the plethora of yachts.

St Tropez would not be what it is today without **Sénéquier, Le Gorille** and the **Café de Paris** – the trendy places overlooking the harbour. If you want to pass as a local you should enter Sénéquier's terrace from the rear. This is where everyone who is anyone meets between 11am and noon. In the early evening it is the ideal spot to watch the mega-yacht owners sipping their cocktails on the aft-deck, and watching you sip yours at Sénequier. At Le Gorille, which even in the 1950s used to stay open right around the clock, André Moraud and his son pull around 45 gallons (200 litres) of beer a day.

La Cave Coopérative has an annual production of 11,000 hectolitres (290,589 gallons) of wine, of which 7,000 are classified as Côtes de Provence AOC. That's 450,000 bottles per year, primarily of rosé – the wine of summer. However, there is also an especially good red, the *Cuvée des Bravades* (for further information contact the tourist office on 94 97 45 21).

In summer St Tropez is pretty well cut-off from the rest of Provence by interminable traffic jams. You are advised to avoid peak hours (such as late afternoon and early evening). Just a few steps from the centre of town there is a mini-airport, with a helicopter service to Nice Airport.

You can get typical country dishes at **Lou Révélen** (4 rue des Ramparts; tel: 94 97 06 34) in the old Quartier de la Ponche not far from the town hall. Fuchs, at 7 Rue des Commerçants (Tel: 94 97 01 25) is very popular for its *plat du jour*. The restaurant **Palmyre** (2 rue Petit-Bal; tel: 94 97 43 22) is located in the heart of St Tropez, but it has country charm. **Chez Nano** (tel: 94 97 01 66) directly opposite the town hall, also attracts visitors with its *plat du jour*: traditional cuisine which owes its excellence to use of the freshest produce. It is imperative that you make reservations at all these restaurants.

By the way, the least expensive double rooms are to be had at **Les Lauriers** (Rue de Temple; tel: 94 97 04 88). This ochre-hued villa is located just behind the Place des Lices. On the other hand, the most beautiful hotel in St Tropez is without doubt the lovely **La Ponche** (Place Cavaillon; tel: 94 97 02 53) which is in the old fishing quarter.

The Beaches

Plage des Graniers: Easily reached on foot.

Bay of Canébeirs: Surrounded by steep cliffs.

Tamaris Beach: In the region of Brigitte Bardot's villa.

Plage des Salins: 2½ miles (4km) east of St Tropez (from there you can take an attractive footpath around the peninsula).

Plage de Tahiti: Gained its name after being used as the Tahitian set for a film directed by René Clair; it belongs to Ramatuelle village.

Plage de Pampelonne: A 3 mile (5km) long beach of fine sand; also belonging to Ramatuelle.

Plage de L'Escalet: Cliffs and sand.

AROUND St TROPEZ

22. Where the Crickets Chirp

La Croix Valmer; along the coast to Cap Lardier and its beach; the Provençal village of Gassin, the Moulins de Paillas; Ramatuelle. (Round-trip about 25 miles/40km. Allow three hours.)

Departing from St Tropez you take the D98a to La Foux and then turn left onto the D559. Because of its mild climate, **La Croix Valmer** has become a popular health resort. Gently rolling hills overgrown with oaks, pines and eucalyptus trees protect the village and the stately villas from cold winds, also helping the quality of the wines cultivated here. The attractive Bouillabaisse Beach is overcrowded during the summer. The path along the coast to Cap Lardier is a good tip.

Gassin is a typical Provençal village, located a commanding 650ft (200m) above the Gulf of St Tropez. **Les Moulins de Paillas** were still operating as mills until the turn of the century; now they are a popular destination for outings and afford wonderful 360° views.

Ramatuelle, on a hill surrounded by vineyards, is a little known secret for all those who find St Tropez too crowded. The village has been shaped by three historical events: the occupation by the Saracens in AD892, almost total destruction in 1592 because of religious conflicts between Catholics and the Protestant Henry IV, and World War II. Because he spoke English, Jean-Pierre Aumont (*see itinerary on St-Tropez, page 98*), was sought out by the American forces landing on Pampelonne to help them make contact with the *Résistance Ramatuelloise,* and so the residents of Cavalaire, La Croix-Valmer and Cogolin had the chance to see their film idol in person – in a Jeep surrounded by GIs.

Today the actor Jean-Claude Brialy creates quite a furore as the artistic director of the **Festival Gérard Philippe**, which has been held annually since 1984. (Philippe's grave is in the Ramatuelle cemetery; the book his wife wrote about the last months they spent together is well worth reading). Brialy has an admirable knack of combining work and pleasure: he has an apartment in one of the twisting alleyways, he breakfasts in the **Café des Ormeaux**, and dines at the **Plage Verte** or the **Mooréa**.

Those who know the 'naked facts' of the local beaches would scarcely be surprised to learn that 'Emmanuelle' – alias Sylvia Kristel – has settled near Pampelonne Beach with her husband.

Leave Ramatuelle by the D61, then turn left onto the D93 which follows the vineyards above Pampelonne Bay. The **Chapelle St Anne** is located in the shade of huge trees on a volcanic cone to our right. The little road, into which we make a right turn to reach the chapel, leads back to St Tropez.

POSTES

HEURES
DES LEVÉES

JOURS OUVRABLES

11H

SAMEDI

10H

BUREAU
LE PLUS PROCHE

ST. PAUL

NE PAS JETER DE JOURNAUX
DANS CETTE BOITE

Dining Exper

Jacques Médecin, once the region's most powerful man but now disgraced, is also the author of a cookery book entitled *Cuisine Niçoise*, which just goes to show what an important rôle the kitchen plays in French society. The former mayor of Nice ended his political career in September 1990 – he resigned and fled to South America. I can't judge the merit of the warrant that was subsequently issued for his arrest, but his cook book can hold its own in this country of gourmets.

Fortunately, after a recent, but thankfully brief, flirtation with *nouvelle cuisine*, the master chefs of the Riviera, of whom there are quite a few, have returned to traditional regional recipes. In order to help you decipher the menus, and make the most of the local dishes, several of the best specialities are listed below.

Pissaladière is a delicious onion pie, flavoured with anchovy purée (*pissala*) and local black olives. *Socca* is a type of thin pancake made of chick pea flour. For *ratatouille* the individual vegetables

(tomatoes, aubergines, red and green peppers, and courgettes) are cooked separately and shouldn't be mixed together until immediately before serving. *Tourte de bléa* is a type of salty pie which is filled with beet greens, currants and almonds or pine nuts.

Salade niçoise, if properly prepared, must consist of salad greens, cucumber slices, tomatoes, black olives, hard-boiled eggs, onions, tuna fish and anchovy filets.

Mesclun is a hearty-tasting salad which absolutely must include dandelion and hedge-mustard leaves. *Petits farcis* are artichoke hearts, baby courgettes and tomatoes with a spicy minced-meat filling which are served *gratiné*. The delicious *beignets des courgettes* are courgette flowers dipped in butter and deep fried, a true delicacy, and one of the world's rare flavours. *Tripe à la niçoise* is prepared with

tomatoes, carrots and lots of garlic. It is the one tripe dish that even dedicated adversaries should taste. *Stocaficada* is a stew of dried codfish – trying it takes a good deal more courage.

Everything which has *pistou* in its name has to do with basil, the ubiquitous herb of the Mediterranean summer. For example, a vegetable soup is transformed when a paste of basil, garlic and olive oil is added. This is equally true of pâtés and pasta. The latter is mixed with pistou and topped off with parmesan cheese. *Gnocchi, ravioli* and pizza taste just as good here as in Italy. *Daube* is large cubes of beef cooked until tender over a low flame in red wine with cinnamon and lemon peel. *Pan bagnant* – white bread soaked with olive oil and layered with greens, onions, tomatoes, hard-boiled eggs and tuna fish – is also sold on the beaches and is a refreshing delicacy in the heat of the mid-afternoon. *Violets* are the small young artichokes without which no crudité basket is worth its name; they are eaten raw. *Aïoli* is a garlic-flavoured mayonnaise; it is served on Fridays with boiled fish and vegetables, a gesture to the days of the Catholic past when everyone ate fish on Friday.

Soup de poisson is a fish-soup with its own ritual: rub the croutons with the garlic cloves that are served with them, lay them in the dish, place a spoonful of the delicious *rouille* (mayonnaise with garlic and pimentos) on top, sprinkle cheese over it and finally pour the soup on top of the lot. A really well-prepared *bouillabaisse*, a medley of fish and flavours, is a true speciality and is only found in a few restaurants. Because it involves numerous fresh ingredients it is not cheap, or easy to make – but it's a pleasure you shouldn't deny yourself.

The tastiest Mediterranean fish are sea-bass (*loup*), John Dory (*St-Pierre*), silver bream and red mullet (*rouget*); the latter should only be ordered filleted, since it has an unbelievable number of bones. Mussels and shellfish should only be eaten from September to April unless you know the restaurant *very* well.

The lamb in this area bears no resemblance whatsoever to the strong-smelling mutton stew which has ruined the pleasure of many in this delicious meat. Since the sheep eat the herbs and spices of Provence the dishes (such as *gigot* – leg of lamb, and *agneau de Sisteron*) taste simply marvellous.

Wine

Provence is known for its rosé wines, which form the greater part of the production, and which are so delicious drunk chilled in the heat of the Mediterranean sun. Côtes de Provence wines were admitted to AOC (Appellation d'Origine Contrôlée status) in 1977. Other AOC wines in the area include Cassis and Bandol, which are situated between Toulon and Marseille, Palette, produced just outside Aix-en-Provence, and Bellet, which is produced on the hills rising directly behind Nice.

AOC is a controlled designation of origin which, within a certain region, regulates the type of grapes, the maximum output, the minimum alcohol content and the number of vines per given area. On the label, the name of the region is printed in large letters along with the words Appellation Contrôlée. VDQS means Vin Délimité de Qualité Supérieure and denotes wines of better quality from certain precisely defined areas. These rank just behind the AOC wines under French law.

Recommended wines to drink with fish and shellfish dishes are Cassis, an excellent dry white (which some say is the only wine to serve with *bouillabaisse*), Bellet, dry yet fruity, or Palette. There are a great many red wines: those from Bandol and the north side of the Massif des Maures are rounded and hearty, while the more elegant and finer ones come from around St Tropez and the Argens Valley.

Domaine means that the wine comes from vineyards which may extend over a very large area. *Château* means a castle or estate winery. If the label indicates that the wine was bottled on the domaine or at the castle, you can be reasonably certain it is a good wine. *Vin de pays* is a simple wine of the region.

A full range of Provençal wines can be tasted and bought at the Maison des Vins, on the main road just outside Les Arcs-sur-Argens (tel: 94 73 33 38). Wines from the following vineyards, many of which can be visited, are sold throughout the region:

Bellet

CHATEAU DE CRÉMAT, St Roman de Bellet

Bandol

DOMAINE OTT, La Londe les Maures
CHATEAU VANNIERES, La Cadière d'Azur
CHATEAU PIBARNON, La Cadière d'Azur

Cassis

CLOS STE MAGDALEINE

Côtes de Provence

CHATEAU MINUTY, Gassin
DOMAINE D'ASTROS, near Vidauban
DOMAINE DE LA BASTIDE BLANCHE, Ramatuelle

Palette

Chateau Simone Palette, Meyreuil

Coteaux d'Aix

Chateau du Seuil, Aix-en-Provence
Comanderie de la Bargemone, RN7, St Cannat
Chateau Vignelaure, Route de Jonques, Rians

Beverage

Coffee and tea aficionados will make good use of the following catalogue, which takes all the confusion, but none of the variety, out of ordering beverages in France: **café noir** is black coffee served in small cups; **café crème** is coffee with steamed milk, served in medium-sized cups; **café au lait** is a large cup of coffee with a lot of steamed milk, usually drunk by the local people only in the mornings; **café décaféiné** is, as the name suggests, decaffeinated coffee. **Thé au citron** is tea with lemon; **thé au lait** is tea with milk; **tisane** is herbal tea; **infusion de camomille** is camomile tea; **infusion de menthe** is peppermint tea.

The French for beer is **bière**; **bière blonde** is light beer or lager; **bière brune** is dark beer; although it doesn't really equate to the British 'bitter'; **bière à la pression** is draught beer; **un bock** is a small glass of beer and **panaché**: beer with soda.

Calendar of Special Events

JANUARY

Mandelieu: Mimosa festival.
Monaco: Festival of Ste-Dévote (Monaco's patron saint). On the evening of 26 January a boat is set ablaze in front of the Ste-Dévote Church; 27 January sees the Monaco Auto-Rally.
Cannes: MIDEM – international music business market.

FEBRUARY

Cannes: Mimosa festival.
Menton: Lemon festival (the two weeks around Shrove Tuesday).
Valbonne: Olive and grape festival.
Nice: Carnival; begins three weeks before Shrove Tuesday (*Mardi Gras*) and ends on Ash Wednesday.

MARCH

Nice: Cougourdon folklore festival in Cimiez.
Roquebrune/Cap Martin: Good Friday evening sees the Procession of the Dead Christ.
Antibes/Juan-les-Pins: Antiques fair.
Vence: Easter Sunday and Monday: Provençal folklore with flower parade.
Fréjus: Third weekend after Easter – *Bravade* in honour of St Francis.

APRIL

Cannes: International Antiques Fair.
Monaco/Nice: International Tennis Tournaments.

MAY

Cannes: International Film Festival.
Nice: Annual parish fair in Cimiez.
Grasse: Provençal folklore, second weekend in May; Rose Festival.
St Tropez: 16–18: *Bravades*.
Monaco: Sunday after Ascension Day: Formula 1 Grand Prix.

JUNE

St Tropez: 15: Spanish *Bravade*.
Nice: Religious music festival.
Cannes: Festival of *Café Théâtre*.

JULY

Nice: The Great Jazz Parade; International folklore festival; flower battle.

Le Cannet: Flower parade.
Cagnes Sur Mer: Evening trotting races at the Hippodrome.
Antibes/Juan-les-Pins: World Jazz Festival.
Cannes: Musical evenings in the Suquet Quarter.
Menton: Fireworks display on 14 July to celebrate Bastille Day; Musical evenings in Pian Park.
Ile Ste-Marguerite: *Son et Lumière* (until September).
Cap d'Antibes: Mariners' festival, marked by a procession to the Church at La Garoupe.
Monaco: Concert in the Courtyard of the Prince's Palace; International Fireworks Festival.
St Tropez: Musical evenings in the Citadel.
Villefranche: Evening performances in the Citadel.

AUGUST

Grasse: First Sunday: Jasmine Festival.
Cannes: Fireworks on 15 August.
Roquebrune/Cap Martin: Procession through the old quarter.
Menton: Chamber music festival (held in the open-air on the plaza of St Michael's Church).

SEPTEMBER

Cannes: Old-timer Festival (vintage cars).
Peille: First Sunday: festival commemorating the ending of a great water shortage.
St Tropez: La Nioulargue (an international sailing competition).

OCTOBER

Nice: Golf tournament; triathlon.

NOVEMBER

Nice: Golf tournament; plus a number of trade fairs, including 'Sea, Mountain and Leisure' fair; antiques fair, furniture and interior design fair.

DECEMBER

Nice: Golf tournament; Christmas swim, when hardy residents brave a communal dip in the sea.
Monaco: International Circus Festival is held.
Lucéram: 24th: the traditional Shepherds' Christmas (to the sound of tambourines and pipes, blessing of the lambs and fruits).

Celebrities on the move

109

Practical Information

Getting Around

Railway Stations (SNCF)

Nice: Tel: 93 87 50 50.
Cannes: Tel: 93 99 50 50.
Marseille: Tel: 91 08 50 50.

Airports

Nice: Tel: 93 21 30 12.
Marseille: Tel: 42 78 21 00.

Helicopter Service

Héli Air Monaco/Héliport de Monaco
Private flights arranged to Nice, Cannes and St Tropez.
Tel: 92 05 00 50.
Héli Transport
Nice: Tel: 93 21 42 00.
Cannes: Tel: 93 90 40 27.
St Tropez: Tel: 94 97 36 45.

Useful Information

Business Hours

Large department stores and shopping centres are open weekdays 10am–noon and 3–7pm. Most food stores are closed 12.30–4pm. Shops on the market streets are open on Sunday and holidays until 12.30pm. Many are closed on Monday. State museums are closed Tuesday and holidays; churches are frequently closed from noon–2pm. Many museums and some hotels are closed in November.

Electrical Equipment

Local current is 220 volts, with two-pin plugs.

Tipping

Gratuities are usually included in the bill in hotels, restaurants and cafés; nonetheless it is customary to give an extra *pourboire*. Barbers and hair stylists, taxi drivers, porters and doormen expect a small tip.

Annual Sales

Winter: 2 January–28 February.
Summer: 15 July–15 September.

Money Matters

Banks

Banks are open Mondays to Fridays 8.30–noon and 1.30–4.30pm. Travellers' cheques and Eurocheques can only be cashed with a passport or other form of personal identification.

The following *bureaux de change* are also open on Sunday and holidays: **Bureau de l'Agence Cook** in the Nice railway station, the **Bureau de Change** in Nice Airport and the **Office Provençal** (Nice, 10 Rue de France).

Credit Cards

American Express, Visa (Carte Bleu) Eurocard, Diners Club and Mastercard are the most frequently honoured. You can't use cards in markets or in many small hotels and restaurants.

Communications and Media

Telephone

Most public telephones require a telephone card available at post offices and tobacco shops.

To dial other countries first dial the international access code 19, wait for the second bleep, then the country code: Australia (61); Ireland (353); UK (44); US and Canada (1). If using a US credit phone card, dial the company's access number below, then 01, then the country code. Sprint, Tel: 19 0087; AT&T, Tel: 19 0011; MCI, Tel: 19 00 19.

Post Offices (PTT)

The *Bureaux de Poste* are open Monday–Friday from 8am–7pm (some from 9am–noon and 2–5pm) and on Saturday from 8am–noon.

Newspapers and Magazines

Nice Matin is the regional daily newspaper. You can also get the *Interna-*

tional Herald Tribune in the morning. The *Guardian* is printed in Marseille; other foreign language newspapers are available by the afternoon. *La Semaine et des Spectacles* and *7 jours 7 nuits* are weekly guides to events and performances. English language publications include the *Riviera Reporter* newspaper and the *Blue Coast* magazine, both monthly.

Radio and Television

Radio Riviera (106.3 FM) is an English language station broadcasting from Monte-Carlo. It buys in BBC World Service programmes. Radio France Internationale has news in English (89 FM). Many hotels have Sky News and CNN. Some foreign films are shown in their original language on French TV and on Télévision Monte-Carlo.

Public Holidays

1 January	New Year's Day
Easter Monday	No fixed date
1 May	Labour Day
8 May	Armistice Day (1945)
Ascension	No fixed date
Pentecost	No fixed date
14 July	Bastille Day
15 August	Assumption
1 November	All Saints' Day
11 November	Armistice Day (1918)
25 December	Christmas Day

Emergencies

Police: Tel: 17
Fire Department: Tel: 18
Ambulance: Tel 15
Lost credit cards
Visa/Mastercard/Carte Bleu:
Tel: 54 42 12 12
American Express:
Tel: 16 1 4777 72 00

On the Road

Driving

The use of safety belts is mandatory in France. Similarly motorcycle riders must wear helmets.
Speed Limits: in-town 60kmh (38mph); on normal roads 90kmh (56mph); on motorways (*autoroutes*) 130kmh (80mph). The motorways are generally toll roads. If you have coins follow the signs reading *automatique*.

In the case of accidents which only involve damage to property, try to avoid a shouting match and fill out the *constat à l'amiable* insurance form. It should be noted that the price of petrol is very high in France.

Maps

Detailed, large-scale maps, useful for walking and cycling, are published by the Institut Géographique Nationale (IGN). The est scale series is 10cm to 1km.

Hotels

The individualists among you will prize the smaller hotels since they have a more personal touch and can make your stay a really memorable experience. My selection is limited to such hotels. Lists of other hotels, including the international chains, with prices and information, are available from tourist offices, both abroad and on the Côte.

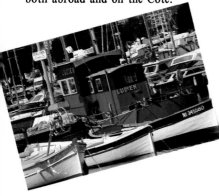

Tourist offices devide the hotels into five categories:

☆☆☆☆☆	Top class luxury hotel
☆☆☆☆	Luxury hotel
☆☆☆	Very comfortable hotel
☆☆	Comfortable hotel
☆	Moderate hotel

The majority of rooms are still furnished with a *grand lit* – a large double-bed. Since you pay for the room and not for the number of persons staying, two people can stay for the price of one – but one person will not be able to pay less than two. Most small and medium-sized hotels have no television in the rooms. The *Guide des Auberges et Hotels de Campagne,* with some 350 addresses throughout France, is recommended for fans of small hotels and country guest-houses.

Price guide:
Inexpensive, less that 400FF
Moderate, 400–750FF
Expensive 750FF.

Antibes

Auberge Provençal,
61 Place Nationale. Tel: 93 34 13 24
Five rooms. Inexpensive.

Cannes

Hôtel Villa Toboso, 7 Allé des Oliviers. Tel: 93 38 20 05
Five minutes from the town centre; 15 rooms with bath. Moderate.

Biot

Galerie des Arcades, 16 Place des Arcades. Tel: 93 65 01 04
12 rooms with bath or shower. Inexpensive.

Vence

La Ferme. Tel: 93 58 74 87
Four rooms with shower. Moderate.

Nice

La Perouse, Quai Raupa Capeu.
Tel: 93 62 34 63
Expensive.
Petit Palais, 10 Avenue Emile Bieckert.
Tel: 93 62 19 11
Moderate.

Grimaud

La Boulangerie. Tel: 94 43 23 16
11 rooms with bath. Inexpensive.

Villefranche sur Mer

Hôtel Welcome, Quai Courbet
Tel: 93 76 76 93.
32 rooms with bath. Expensive.

St Paul de Vence

Le Hameau, Route de la Colle
Tel: 93 32 80 24.
17 rooms with bath. Moderate.

St Jean Cap Ferrat

Brise Marine, 58 Avenue Jean Mermoz
Tel: 93 76 04 36
15 rooms with bath. Moderate.

Mougins

Le Manoir de l'Etang,
Bois de Fontmerle. Tel: 93 90 01 07
13 rooms with bath. Moderate.

St Tropez

Le Pré de la Mer, Route des Salins.
Tel: 94 97 12 23
Three rooms with bath (moderate).
Nine studios equipped with small kitchens (expensive).

Shopping

Nice and Around

In the city centre surrounding the **Place Masséna**, 64 luxury boutiques have come together and designated their neighbourhood the **Carré d'As** (look for the blue-green sign: *Bienvenue au Carré d'As*). They've made quality and outstanding service their bywords. The Avenue Jean Médecin is the main shopping street; it includes the Galeries Lafayette and Nice Etoile. Similarly expensive shops are found in the pedestrian zone in the Rue Masséna/Rue de France.

A flea market is held on Monday on the Cours Saleya between the old quarter and the sea.

The imposing shopping centre CAP 3000 is located just behind the airport. It has countless boutiques – for every budget and taste. In **La Colle sur Loup** there is a street full of antique shops; the boutiques of **Juan-les-Pins** are open until 11pm and later. You can buy beautiful glasses in **Biot** in the Verrerie de Biot. Those who like lithography should take a look at the Fondation Maeght in **St Paul de Vence**.

Cannes and Around

The **Rue d'Antibes** – parallel to the Croisette – is the main shopping street of Cannes. It is often compared with the Rue de Faubourg St-Honoré, and the prices are as inflated here as they are there. Each Saturday there is a flea market with relatively reasonable prices in the **Allées de la Liberté** across from the Palais des Festivals. The **Rue Meynadier** is well known for its food stores.

You can get *eau de toilette* and good soap in **Grasse**, and those who are already thinking of Christmas can buy nativity figures and statues of saints made of unfired clay, called *santons*, in **Cabris** at 18 Rue de la Terrace. Picasso made **Vallauris** famous as a pottery centre; you can buy beautiful majolica in the Galerie Madoura.

Ceramics

The following are recommended outlets for locally-made pots and souvenirs:

Annelise Schäle
Rue du Caïre, 83440 Seillans.
Phillippe Gallot
Poterie du Boutau, Place de la Liberté, 06770 Levens.
Jean-Pierre Faucher
Saint Eloi, 83131 Montferrat.
Albrecht Schönerstedt
Sculptures Céramiques, Pont du Caramy, 83570 Carcès.
Voelkel S & P
83640 St Zacherie.
Roland Moreau
La Barbacasse, Tourettes sur Loup.

Museums

Museum Passes

You can buy a bargain three-day or seven-day Carte Musées Côte d'Azur pass giving entrance to some 58 museums and galleries in the region.

Restaurants

Visiting restaurants on the Côte is a genuine pleasure whether they be gourmet temples or simple bistros. The well-known food guides with which most gourmets are familiar give information on the huge number of options available. However, personal recommendations are just as welcome (if not more so) to the food lover, and the following list is a compilation of my own favourite restaurants. It is essential to make reservations, especially during the high season.

Nice

La Meranda, 4 Rue de la Terrasse.
No telephone. Small, unassuming bistro offering excellent Provençal specialities.
Les Dents de la Mer, 2 Rue St Françoise de Paule. Tel: 93 80 99 16.
Terrace; fish specialities.
L'Esquinade, 5 Quai des Deux-Emmanuels. Tel: 93 89 59 36.
On the old harbour, L'Esquinade offers a cheerful ambience; features fish specialities and great desserts; not cheap.
Grand Café de Turin, Place Garibaldi. Tel: 93 62 29 52. The place for shellfish.

Cannes

Le Mesclun, 16 rue St-Antoine.
Tel: 93 99 45 19. Delicious food at reasonable prices.
Astoux et Brun, 27 Rue Félix Faure. Tel: 93 39 21 87.
Excellent seafood at reasonable prices.

St Jeannet

Auberge de St Jeannet.
Tel: 93 24 90 06.
Rustic ambience, Mediterranean specialities.

Antibes

Restaurant du Bacon, Boulevard du Bacon. Tel: 93 61 50 02.
Terrace; the best fish restaurant on the Côte; expensive.

Au Régal, 5 Rue Sade.
Tel: 93 34 11 69.
Beautiful garden; very good food.
Auberge Provençale, 61 Place Nationale. Tel: 93 34 13 24.
Patio garden; traditional dishes.

Cagnes-sur-Mer

Charlot, 87 Boulevard de la Plage/Cros de Cagnes. Tel: 93 31 00 07.
Serene ambience; very good fish dishes.
Le Picadéro, 3 Boulevard de la Plage/Cros de Cagnes. Tel: 93 73 57 81.
Bistro atmosphere; excellent food.

Juan-les-Pins

Auberge de l'Esterel, 21 Chemin des Iles. Tel: 93 61 86 55.
Beautiful garden; outstanding food.

Biot

Restaurant des Arcades, 15 Place des Arcades. Tel: 93 65 01 04.
Simple country guest-house.
Auberge du Jarrier, 30 Passage de la Bourgade. Tel: 93 63 11 68.
Terrace; extraordinary food.

Valbonne

Le Bistrot de Valbonne, 11 Rue de la Fontaine. Tel: 93 42 05 59.
A small terrace; excellent food.

Vence

La Farigoule, 15 Rue Henri Isnard.
Tel: 93 58 01 27.
Attractive interior courtyard; Provençal specialities.

Grasse

Maître Boscq, 13 Rue de la Fontette.
Tel: 93 36 45 76.
Specialises in traditional cuisine. Reasonable prices.

St Tropez

Baou-Baou, Plage de la Bouillabaise.
Tel: 94 97 18 34.
The chicken with crayfish is especially good.

Le Bistrot des Lices, 3 Place des Lices. Tel: 94 97 29 00.
This is a favourite meeting place for chic Parisians.
La Marjolaine, Rue François Sibilli. Tel: 94 97 04 60.
A rustic *trattoria*. I especially recommend the excellent value *prix fixe* menu.

St Paul de Vence

La Colle-sur-Loup, Hostellerie de l'Abbaye. Tel: 93 32 66 77.
Beautiful courtyard.
La Colombe d'Or, Tel: 93 32 80 02.
Romantic terrace; attracts an illustrious clientele.

Menton

Chez Germaine, 46 Promenade de Maréchel Le-Clerc. Tel: 93 35 66 90.
Very good salmon with sorrel.

Haut-de-Cagnes

Restaurant des Peintres, 71 Montée de la Bourgade. Tel: 93 20 83 08.
The crayfish and salad with roast duck or goose liver are particularly recommended.
Josy Jo, 2 Rue du Planastel. Tel: 93 20 68 76. Attractive garden terrace; excellent food.

Nightlife

Antibes / Juan-les-Pins

Le Bureau, Avenue Galice; Juan-les-Pins. Disco; opens at 11.30pm; admission fee.
La Siesta, La Brague, Route du Bord de Mer.
Seven dance floors; admission fee.
Whisky a Gogo, Juan-les-Pins.
Disco; opens at 11pm; admission fee.

Cannes

Club Otéro, 48 La Croisette; inside the Carlton Hotel. Piano bar/disco. Open from 9pm.
Le Jimmy'z, Palais des Festivals.
Nightclub; opens 11pm.

Nice

Iguane Café, 5 Quai des Deux Emmanuel. Piano bar, restaurant and discotheque. Lively Latin American ambience.
Las Vegas, 10 Rue Maréchal Joffre.
Disco; opens at 10pm.
Jok-Club Disco, 1 Promenade des Anglais. Opens at 11pm.
Offshore, 29 Rue Alphonse Karr.
Disco opens at 11pm; admission fee.
Au Pizzaiolo, 4 Rue du Port Vieux.
Restaurant (features *niçoise* specialities), shows and dancing.
Le Pastel, 41 Quai des Etats-Unis.
Piano bar.

St Tropez

Les Caves du Roy, Hotel Byblos. Tel: 94 97 00 04.
Sumptuous anquets; reserve 1–2 days ahead.
L'Esquinade, Near the city hall.
Disco, opens at 11pm, admission fee.
Le Papagayo, Residence du Port.
Disco, opens at 11pm, admission fee.

Sport

Golf Courses

Biot
Bastide du Roy.
Tel: 93 65 08 48

Cannes
Mandelieu la Napoule.
Tel: 93 49 55 39

La Londe les Maures
Domaine de Valcros.
Tel: 94 66 81 02

Monaco
La Turbie. Tel: 93 41 09 11.
Eze Country Club. Accessible via the D45. Tel: 93 41 24 64

Mougins
175 Route d'Antibes.
Tel: 93 75 79 13

Nice
698 Route de Grenoble
Tel: 93 29 82 00

Roquebrune/Argens
Domaine des Planes
Tel: 94 82 92 91

St Maxime
Route du Débarquement.
Tel: 94 49 26 60

St Raphael
Quartier de Valescure
Tel: 94 82 40 46

Valbonne
Route de Roquefort
Tel: 93 12 21 05

Riding

La Colle sur Loup
Route de Montegros.
Tel: 93 32 68 33

Grasse
Chemin des Mosques
Tel: 93 36 13 23
168 Route de Cannes
Tel: 93 70 55 41

Mandelieu
Club San Estello (N17)
Tel: 93 49 64 74

Nice
Crazy Horse, Route du Mont Leuze
Tel: 93 01 84 11

Roquefort
Chemin Toures
Tel: 93 77 51 64.

St Paul
600 Chemin Malvan
Tel: 93 32 96 34

St Tropez
Domaine de Beauvallon
Tel: 94 56 16 55

Sophia Antipolis
Centre Hippique
Tel: 93 65 32 65

Vence
Col de Vence.
Tel: 93 58 09 83

Villeneuve-Loubet
Route de Grasse.
Tel: 93 20 99 64

Hiking Paths

Le Sentier des Balcons de la Côte d'Azur leads from Menton into the Esterel through more than 100 miles (160km) of glorious countryside (GR51). Hiking guides (*Sentiers Touristiques*) and maps can be bought in bookshops.

Boat Rental

Antibes:
Antibes Yachting Services
Tel: 93 74 30 44
L'Ile Bleue. Tel: 93 34 64 65
Camper et Nicholson
Tel: 92 91 29 12

Cannes:
Camper et Nicholson
Tel: 93 43 16 75
Figurehead. Tel: 92 99 39 93
Marcelle Senesi. Tel: 93 99 03 51

Juan-les-Pins:
Sam Boat Location. Tel: 93 61 23 04
Easy Yachting. Tel: 93 67 75 91

Mandelieu:
Challenge des Mers. Tel: 93 93 12 34

Monaco:
Camper et Nicholson
Tel: 93 50 84 86

Speed Limits

Max speed 5 knots 1,000ft (300m) from the coast; in busy offshore waters (for example near the Lérins Islands and off Villefranche) the maximum is 12 knots.

Markets

Markets are a joy on the Côte d'Azur, especially food and flea markets.

Antibes

Cours Masséna. Daily except Monday, from 6am–noon.

Flea market. Thursday on Place Audiberti.

Handicrafts. Cours Masséna: Tuesday, Thursday, Friday and Sunday starting at 2pm.

Clothing. Place du Tribunal, Tuesday and Saturday; Place Nationale, Thursday.

Cagnes-sur-Mer

Town Centre. Pedestrian zone, daily except Monday.

Cannes

Flower Market. Rue Félix Faure, daily except Monday.

Flea market. Rue Félix Faure, Saturday.

Forville Market and **Rue Maynadier**: daily except Monday.

Grasse

Place aux Aires. Daily except Monday.

Fréjus

Place des Poivriers. Wednesday and Saturday mornings.

Flower Market. Place de la Mairie: Wednesday and Saturday mornings.

Menton

Halles. Daily, except forMonday.

Flea market. Place aux Herbes, Friday.

Clothing market. Halles, Saturday.

Monaco

Condamine Market/Monte Carlo Market. Every morning, except Monday.

Nice

Saleya Market/Liberation Market/Fontaine du Temple Market. Every morning except Monday.

Flea market. Cours Saleya, Monday.

Fish market. Place St Francois, every morning except Monday.

Vence

Little Market. Place Clemenceau, Tuesday mornings.

Large Market. Place Clemenceau, Friday mornings.

Index

NOTES

ACKNOWLEDGMENTS

Design Concept   **V Barl**
Cover Design   **Klaus Geisler**
Cartography   **Berndtson & Berndtson**

ENGLISH EDITION

Production Editor   **Erich Meyer**
Managing Editor   **Dorothy Stannard**

NOTES